CRIME
IN THE
SECOND
WORLD WAR

Spivs, Scoundrels, Rogues and Worse

CRIME
IN THE
SECOND
WORLD WAR
Spivs, Scoundrels, Rogues and Worse

Penny Legg

SABRESTORM

In memory of Mum and Dad,
children of The Second World War,
who both passed away while I was writing this book
and for Joe, who got me through.

Designed and typeset by Philip Clucas MSIAD

British Library Cataloguing in Publication Data

A catalogue record for this book is available from the British Library

Published by Sabrestorm Publishing, 90 Lennard Road, Dunton Green, Sevenoaks, Kent TN13 2UX

Website: www.sabrestorm.com
Email: books@sabrestorm.com

Printed in Malaysia by Tien Wah Press

ISBN 978-1-78122-009-2

Contents

Foreword 7
by Michael O'Bryne QPM,
Chief Constable (Rtd), Bedfordshire Police

Introduction 9

1 Looting 12

2 The Black Market 30

3 Crimes by Black Out 50

4 Murder 62

5 Fraud, Theft, Hooch and
Other Crimes 102

6 Armed Services Crime 122

Epilogue 151

Bibliography 152

Acknowledgements 155

Picture Credits 157

Index 158

For the first time in history the large centres of civilian population were primary targets for an enemy whose aim was to obliterate the means of production and to terrify the population into surrender.

Foreword

Penny Legg has chosen a particularly fascinating time to look at crime in Britain. Given that the 'primary objectives' set for the police by Rowan and Maine, the original Commissioners of Police (as a new organisation with much feared power, the government did not trust it to one acting alone) were 'the protection of life and property', it is easy to see that the all-out war that Hitler raged on Britain was a time of historic challenge for the police. For the first time in history the large centres of civilian population were primary targets for an enemy whose aim was to obliterate the means of production and to terrify the population into surrender.

The police ability to respond was significantly compromised by two other factors. The first was the number of forces, there were over 240, many based on relatively small boroughs and less than 100 in strength. The level of expertise and professionalism in the smaller forces was very poor and most 'stranger' murders were investigated by a team of two detectives, usually a detective chief superintendent and a detective sergeant, sent down from Scotland Yard, complete with their famous murder bag. The second factor was that most of the more able and energetic did their best to get out of the service to join the armed forces.

The effectiveness of the police patrol was based on the fact that the beat officer would see the same scene and the same people day after day. So when something unusual happened or a strange person appeared in the neighbourhood they stuck out. The mass movement of the population either into the armed services or to work in the massively expanded factories knocked that effectiveness on the head. Add to this the sudden arrival in rural areas of large concentrations of men, firstly from all over Britain and then the United States, and the wonder is that the rate of crime stayed so low.

Left: The freak effects of a bursting bomb leave the private open to the world. A bedroom is exposed to the street, and furniture slides to the corner of a crazily suspended floor, but ornaments and a clock remain in their place on a mantelshelf.

Above: 3rd September 1939 and crowds gathered outside Downing Street at 11am to hear the news they dreaded. Britain was at war again. For some, too young to understand the implications, it was exciting to look in wonder at all the people nearby. Others rubbed their hands in glee at the thought of the opportunities to come.

The final difficulty for the police was the combined effect of rationing, the blackout and massive numbers of men without women and under threat of death in action. This created a fertile seedbed for racketeering, prostitution and the men who lived on it, and old-fashioned theft and robbery, all of this providing a viable off-the-books living for the army of deserters (up to 100,000) that is rarely discussed.

Penny Legg's book provides an intriguing insight into a unique episode in British history for any historian and is a wonderful source book for anyone tempted to write a crime fiction based on the period.

Michael O'Byrne QPM
Chief Constable Bedfordshire 1996 -2001

Author of:
Changing Policing; Revolution not Evolution (Russell House Publishing Ltd., 2001), and *The Crime Writers Guide to Police Practice and Procedure* (Robert Hale Ltd., 2009, 2nd Ed. 2015)

The day alerts were so frequent that
it was difficult to remember whether
the last wailing of the siren had been
the alert or the 'all clear'

Barbara Nixon

Introduction

Britain was at war once more. Those who remembered the traumatic years between 1914 and 1918 shivered and braced themselves, gas masks at the ready, for the carnage they had hoped they would never have to experience again. Families were ripped apart as husbands and sons were called up for active service, mothers and daughters stepped into their shoes in the work place and children were banished to the safety of the countryside as evacuees. The lights went out all over Britain, make do and mend became a way of life and living on the ration was an increasing struggle.

Sadly, those left on the home front also learnt to obey a new master, the air raid siren, whose strident call gave warning of looming menace. In London alone there were over seven hundred sirens, positioned strategically for maximum effect. Barbara Nixon, one of the first women to become a full time air raid warden, in her autobiography, *Raiders Overhead, A diary of the London blitz*, (Scolar Press, 1980) comments ten days into the blitz, "The day alerts were so frequent that it was difficult to remember whether the last wailing of the siren had been the alert or the 'all clear'".

In 1942, the American government produced a booklet to help their servicemen understand Great Britain, a quaint country with a long history and baffling traditions. Reproduced as *Welcome to Britain* by Sabrestorm Publishing, it explained that members of the American expeditionary forces in the country were there 'as part of an Allied offensive – to meet Hitler and beat him on his own ground.' It went on to explain some of the puzzling complexities of the British people, their way of life and how they coped living in a war zone. One section graphically brings home to a twenty-first century audience the Britain the Americans arrived to find.

'The houses haven't been painted because factories are not making paint – they're making planes. The famous English gardens and parks are either unkept because there are no men to take care of them, or they are being used to grow needed vegetables. British taxicabs look antique because Britain makes tanks for herself and Russia and hasn't time to make new cars. British trains are cold because power is needed for industry, not for heating. There are no luxury dining cars on trains because total war effort has no place for such frills. The trains are unwashed and grimy because men and women are needed for more important work than car-washing.'

This gives an impression of a people totally immersed in its war effort, with everyone pulling together to do their bit for their country in its time of need. Whilst it is undoubtedly true that most did do as much as possible to help, the picture was not all rosy.

Crime, unfortunately, did not go away during the crisis Britain found itself in during the first half of the 1940s. Rather, new opportunities presented themselves and the unscrupulous took full advantage. At the outbreak of war, the government opened the prison doors to all who had less than three months to serve, and all Borstal lads who had served more than six months. If these criminals were not called up immediately, they were free to capitalise on the conditions they found on the outside. There were those who looked on war as an opportunity, either to make a quick profit, to settle old scores or to use the conditions of the time for their own gain.

While the country made sure to observe the blackout, so that there were few lights by which German bombers could see their targets, burglars used the cover of darkness to tiptoe into premises and help themselves. The ruins of bombed out buildings became ideal hiding places for the corpses of murder victims, or were picked over by looters. In the meantime, local gangs took full advantage and gang warfare or organised crime gave the police of the period more to worry about. The large numbers of service personnel in the country, both British and from overseas, brought with them their own problems, sometimes leading to violent crimes, such as rape or murder. Sadly, too, those with previously unblemished reputations found themselves tempted off the straight and narrow and so-called 'white collar crime' rocketed. As historian Simon Read comments, 'Rationing, blackouts and the severe limitations under which the police worked all came together to create a criminal's paradise.' (*Dark City, Crime in Wartime London*, 2010)

This book looks at some of the crime reported during the dark days of World War Two. It is not meant to be a comprehensive listing of every misdemeanour that occurred or a treatise on the subject. Rather, it is a taste of some of the different crimes that were committed, how they were detected and what happened to those involved and is designed to be dipped into. The reader will gain an idea of another side to the British home front. Sadly, it is an impression that casts a dark cloud over the perception that 'everyone pulled together' during the war years.

Penny Legg   2016

Above: "If you see a queue... join it!" Housewives form an ordely line for horse flesh.

Above: Aldwich Underground station proves safe shelter during the London Blitz.

Relief at surviving was sometimes
tempered by the loss of a sentimental
object, not through an action by an
overseas and unseen enemy but by
an unscrupulous home front one.

1

Looting –
The Enemy at Home

The Concise Oxford Dictionary variously defines '***loot***' as:
Noun – 1 goods taken from an enemy; spoil. 2 booty; illicit gains
made by an official.
Verb – rob (premises) or steal (goods) left unprotected, esp. after
riots or other violent events.

The eight months, one week and two days of the German blitz, between 7
September 1940 and 21 May 1941, produced startling statistics. The
Luftwaffe succeeded in dropping more than one hundred tonnes of
explosives on sixteen cities throughout Britain. More than 40,000 people
were killed and up to 139,000 more were injured. London endured fifty-
seven consecutive nights of bombing by the German air force and 1,150,000
houses were damaged. Coventry town centre was flattened. In Hull, of
93,000 homes, only 6,000 escaped completely.

In Southampton, German aeroplanes tried to hit the Supermarine
factory on the River Itchen, which was the home of the Spitfire, and the
Vosper Thornycroft naval shipyard a short distance from it. There were
several botched bombing attempts, during which may parts of the town
were devastated. These including the nearby residential area of Woolston,
where the damage was to the point where the destroyed homes were later
used as a troop training ground for war-ravaged conditions in France in the
run up to D-Day.

Having their premises bombed was bad enough but just when
householders were at their lowest ebb, having lost family, their home or

Above: The Spitfire was built on the banks of the River Itchen in Woolston,
Southmpton, at the Supermarine factory – a target for the Luftwaffe.

business to enemy bombing, there was sometimes more heartache in store for them. Empty, derelict or bomb damaged properties were a draw for the unscrupulous. Families, prevented from returning to their properties by any number of continuing hazards - air raids; unexploded ordnance; the perilous state of their own or neighbouring buildings; gas or water leaks to name just a few - often finally returned to what was left of their homes to find that their undamaged possessions had been rifled through and stolen. Relief at surviving was sometimes tempered by the loss of a sentimental object, not through an action by an overseas and unseen enemy but by an unscrupulous home front one. The realisation that there were those prepared to help themselves to other people's possessions during such dire times was often a shock for the victims. As Norman Longmate notes, 'What the bombs had left, the looters often got,' (*How We Lived Then*, 1971). It was this home front betrayal that often broke the spirit of otherwise dauntless people. Looting became so prevalent that by November 1940 the *Daily Mail* was proclaiming: 'Hang a looter and stop this filthy crime.'

Coventry

Edgar Storer, quoted in *The Gentlemen at War* (Roy Ingleton, 1994) was a Walsall Borough Policeman. He was part of a contingent of twenty-five officers bussed into Coventry immediately after the city was ravaged, on 14 November 1940, to provide emergency assistance. He was there for two weeks. He notes that, despite the widespread destruction, the city's population went on as usual and 'there was practically no looting.' This, sadly, was not the state of affairs in many towns and was eventually not found to be the case in Coventry. Eager sightseers flocked to the city to witness the carnage and perhaps pick up a souvenir while they were there. When 800 money-in-the-slot prepayment gas and electricity meters were removed from bombed premises in the city in December 1940, they were found to have been broken into and emptied. Some of the meter looters were identified as members of the armed forces, stationed nearby and at a loose end after being told to stand down and wait for orders rather than help with the clean-up efforts.

Defence Regulations

Looting was not originally specified in the Defence Regulations, put together at the start of the war under The Emergency Powers (Defence) Act in 1939, or its successor, The Emergency Powers (Defence) Act, 1940. These acts allowed the Defence Regulations to cover as many of the foreseen problems that might occur during wartime as possible. In practice, they governed most aspects of life. In time, they were widely seen as increasingly intrusive on everyday life, with regulations covering such minutiae as, for example,

Both above: The ruins of Coventry Cathedral, casualty of the Coventry blitz on 14 November 1940. It is shown as it was on the day after the devastation (top), and as the war-ravaged cathedral appears today (above).

Above: In the midst of clearing up after a bombing raid, looting from bombed-out shops could be easy, providing rich pickings for the unscrupulous.

the direction in which a car should be parked. Inevitably, gaps came to light as the war progressed and there were numerous additions to the regulations as time went by. Looting was one such addition. It was covered by Regulation 38a, amended in October 1940 to allow looters to be punished with the death penalty. This, on paper at least, brought it into line with German laws – looters there being shot if caught. Notices soon appeared in bombed-out British shop premises announcing:

Warning!
Looting from premises, which have been damaged by or vacated by reason of war operations, is punishable by death or penal servitude for life.

As Peter Lewis, in his Channel Four book, *A People's War* (1986) points out, these punishments were never enforced, but, nevertheless, they were there and could have been used if necessary, particularly if an example needed to be made to deter others.

As Mr Justice Charles of the Leeds Assizes commented, on 5 March 1941 after two full days of trying looters from Sheffield, by making looting punishable by the death sentence, the law was putting the crime on a par with murder, which carried the same punishment (*An Underworld at War*, Donald Thomas, 2003).

An Opportunity

Opportunist thieves seemed to be everywhere and were sometimes people who were known and trusted by their victims. The *Yorkshire Evening Post* on 19 September 1940 reported the case of thirty-eight-year-old Mrs Mabel Burgess, who took the chance an air raid afforded to steal £3 7s from her next door neighbour. For her trouble, she was sentenced to twenty-eight days' imprisonment at the South-western Police Court. Donald Thomas (*An Underground at War*) mentions the plight of Mrs Mary May in Camberwell, whose house was bombed out in the blitz in 1940. She stayed with friends until she could return to the house, by which time her neighbour had plundered her home, including her piano and sewing machine.

Above: The devastation caused by a V2 rocket shows the extent of damage - and the huge opportunity for looting.

Plans made for what to do with those who had survived being bombed-out were woefully inadequate in many areas. Rest Centres were often school halls, with buckets and coalscuttles for toilets. Food was sparse and poor, and washing facilities almost non-existent. Barbara Nixon, in her wartime memoirs *Raiders Overhead, A diary of the London Blitz* (1980), mentions that a friend volunteered to help out at a dockside area soon after a raid. More than a thousand people needing medical and other practical help were at the Town Hall. The local authority produced £30 as its relief fund. It was enough to buy 'an inadequate supply of tea … and no food!' Nixon also cites the example of one family who had to traipse through pouring rain to five different Rest Centres to find money, clothes and cups of tea after being bombed out, as each distribution in the area had been centralised. Two of the family had only carpet slippers for footwear. As Peter Lewis points out, the authorities had expected no one to live in the event of aerial bombardment, so what to do with

Rest Centres were often school halls, with buckets and coalscuttles for toilets.

filthy, cold and hungry survivors was a problem. In such a situation, everything has a value, as the letter from an indignant 'Air-raid Victim' printed in the *Sunderland Daily Echo and Shipping Gazette* for 26 November 1940, shows. The writer complains that police have not caught the person who removed the sink from his bombed-out house.

No Fear …

Raynes Minns, in her informative *Bombers & Mash* (1980), noted that the peak time for looting was in the lull period between the sounding of the air raid siren and the first detonation. Simon Read, (*Dark City, Crime in Wartime London*, 2010) echoes this view and says that there was 'little fear of capture' during the raids themselves. Gavin Mortimer noted that the moment the sirens sounded the looters were 'slithering unseen' about their work (*The Longest Night,* 2005). Thus, if you had the nerve, an air raid was literally a heaven-sent opportunity for some. Nothing was left behind and everything from cutlery to clothing, jewellery to coal was stripped from premises – homes, shops, churches and factories – often by organised gangs. Read quotes the example of Dover, many of whose inhabitants had been evacuated because the town's proximity to France brought it within easy range of enemy guns and aircraft. Some returning evacuees found that

Right: After the air raid, what was left of the family's possessions were often piled up outside their ruined home. This made looting very convenient for the light-fingered.

Above: *Plymouth endured 59 bombing raids between 1941 and 1944, during which 3,754 houses were completely destroyed and 18,398 were damaged. Salvaged possessions were often left out in the street after being saved from the ruins of family homes, as here, in a photograph taken after the raid on the night of 20th and 21st March 1941. Such treasure troves provided rich pickings for looters.*

the only things still in their homes when they arrived were the blackout curtains. It was later found that London gangs had brought in vans with local removal company liveries printed on their sides, so as not to arouse suspicion about their activities, and literally moved out anything that was portable, including prising up stair carpets and manoeuvring mangles. It does not take much to realise the hardship this caused to low income families.

No Shame …

Some people did not seem to regard what they had done as being wrong. The *Yorkshire Evening Post* and other newspapers of 29 August 1940 has a brief mention of the case of thirty-two-year-old Ivy Stephens, who was charged with stealing a little girl's dress from a house wrecked during an air raid. The raid had killed the child who owned the dress. The newspaper reports that Stephens said when charged: "I didn't steal it. I thought it would do for my little girl."

All looting was frowned upon but none more so than that perpetrated by members of trusted bodies: the rescue services such as the Fire Service; the

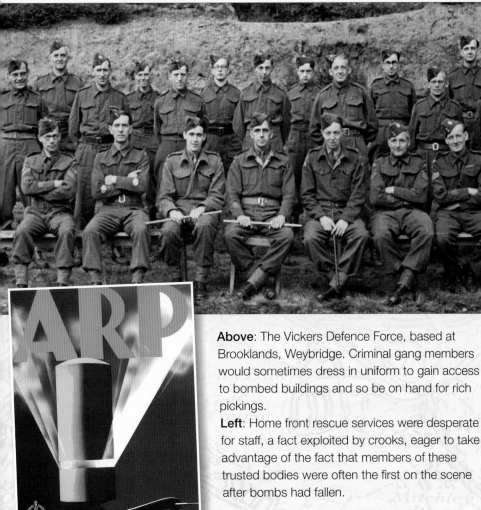

Above: The Vickers Defence Force, based at Brooklands, Weybridge. Criminal gang members would sometimes dress in uniform to gain access to bombed buildings and so be on hand for rich pickings.

Left: Home front rescue services were desperate for staff, a fact exploited by crooks, eager to take advantage of the fact that members of these trusted bodies were often the first on the scene after bombs had fallen.

Police; Air Raid Wardens; the Home Guard and other groups who might have been expected to keep their fingers to themselves. Determined thieves would volunteer for those positions that offered the best opportunity of rich pickings and what better place for first option on what lay inside ruined buildings than those who were first on the scene? Paul Lunde mentions looters dressed in ARP uniforms, who were so convincing that the public were fooled into helping them empty ruined premises (*Organised Crime, An Inside Guide to the World's Most Successful Industry*, 2004). The *Sunderland Daily Echo and Shipping Gazette* on 2 October 1940 reports the cases of two London Auxiliary Firemen, Charles Herbert Palmer, 36, and Clarence Foxcroft, 31, who, while engaged in firefighting in the city's West End, took the opportunity to pocket small items from the premises they were supposed to be protecting. Palmer was seen to pick up a cigarette lighter from the scattered fragments and when confronted was found to have other such items on him, to the value of £6 12s 6d (£6.62). He was sent for trial for looting at the Central Criminal Court and was refused bail. Foxcroft was also seen to pocket items from the wreckage. The newspaper stated that his defence was that he had been working sixty hours a week as a volunteer fireman and his work in rescuing people from damaged buildings was reportedly good. Perhaps it was this previous good character that led to the lesser charge of theft being made against him. He was found guilty and sentenced to four months in jail with hard labour.

Startling Statistics

Within two months of the beginning of the London blitz, newspapers as far away from the capital as Scotland (*Aberdeen Journal*, 31 October 1940) were reporting startling statistics on air raid looting. There had been 390 cases of looting brought before Bow Street Police Court in September and October 1940. These, the newspaper stated, cast 'a slur on fine men' not involved.

Christmas is a time when hardship can be difficult to bear. In an age when rationing was becoming the norm and trying to continue pre-war traditions such as gift giving was increasingly hard, the actions of one member of the Home Guard can perhaps be understood, if not excused. The *Hartlepool Mail* of 9 December 1940 recounts the story of forty-five-year-old William Banker, from London's Southall area. Banker, described as a railway shopman, was attached to the Passenger Transport Board. Part of his job was, he said, to prevent looting. It was somewhat surprising then for him to be seen going to a bombed out sweet shop and helping himself to two jars of confectionary, which he put inside his overcoat.

The Café de Paris

In London, the gay Café de Paris in Piccadilly was the haunt of choice of the upper ten thousand, including military officers, the rich and the famous. It was a place for those who could afford it to forget that there was a war on; where they could dine, dance and enjoy their champagne. The entertainment was first class and it had a fine reputation for being *the* place to be. The tradition continues today. The café's website explains that it was opened in 1924 and soon patronised by royalty, becoming a favourite nightspot of the Prince of Wales. It became a place 'to see and be seen' in. The 1929 film *Piccadilly* used the café as its backdrop and Cole Porter introduced the world to new songs at the café in the 1930s. At the outbreak

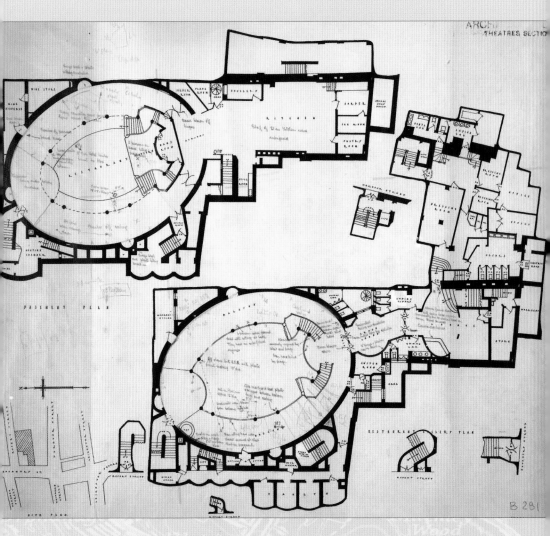

Above: The Café de Paris was said to be impervious to enemy bombs but this was to be proved wrong on 8 March 1941. This map shows the damage and casualties caused by bombing that night. Looters soon appeared.

of war, such was the reputation of the Café de Paris that it was allowed to stay open when most of the other such venues in the city were closed down. As the café's websites says, 'People gossiped their way through the blackout, safe in the knowledge that the venue was impervious to the bombing outside.' This was a view put about by Martinus Poulsen, the restaurant's self-made maitre d', who, it was said by friends, "Smiled his way to fortune." Poulsen argued that the solid four storeys of the café building would offer protection from anything that the enemy could throw at it.

Above: Death on the Dance Floor. Clearing debris from the Cafe de Paris where guests and members of the band were killed by a direct hit.

   Sadly, this view might have been popular but it was to prove to be disastrously wrong. On 8 March 1941, at the height of the London Blitz, the Café de Paris was hit. It was Services Night and as such, the room was full of military men and women having fun. Newspapers up and down the land later reported on the bombing, which was to lead to ATS Private Marjorie Price being mentioned in Army Orders for her conspicuous gallantry that evening. She had had shoes that pinched her and this had led to her vacating the dance floor just as the bombs hit, a move which may have saved her life. *The Dundee Evening Telegraph*, on Saturday 5 April 1941, reported that shortly after a performance by twenty-seven-year-old Ken 'Snake Hips' Johnson and his West Indian Orchestra, a bomb fell through the ceiling and hit the balcony just above the musicians. The *Sunday Post* states that two bombs hit the café, a view which is echoed on the Café de Paris website. The carnage from a falling staircase and ceiling, glass flying and the 'avalanche of debris' was devastating, although from the outside of the building nothing could be seen of the damage. 'Snake Hips' and most of his band were killed, along with forty-seven-year-old Mr Poulsen himself. The dead, the injured and the confused littered the restaurant and there was widespread shock at what had happened. The manager of the hotel opposite the Café de Paris, Albert Weaver, who was also a member of the Home Guard, told reporters that he had led a band of hotel residents and staff by torchlight to help rescue the injured. "Everyone worked marvellously and those trapped in the building had been released before midnight," he is quoted as saying. "Girl members of the staff made tea and everything was done to make them comfortable." One of the walking wounded commented that, "soldiers with field dressings" arrived to help other rescue workers tend to the injured. The picture conjured up of the scene is one of Londoners looking after their own after a devastating event.

However, there was one group of locals who were looking after themselves rather than anyone else at the Café de Paris. An unnamed but often mentioned off duty nurse from Chelsea, whose work that evening was universally praised, later commented that while she had been busy tending the wounded, her handbag had been rifled and several items, including a fountain pen, had been taken.

The actor, Ballard Berkeley, born Ballard Blascheck, (1904 – 1988) remembered with affection as Major Gowan in the television series *Fawlty Towers*, was a Special Constable in London during this period. Gavin Mortimer quotes him, in his book, *The Longest Night, 10 – 11 May 1941 Voices From The London Blitz*, (2005) and in his later article *A Nation of looters: it even happened in the Blitz* (2011) in *The Week* online. Berkeley mentions the fact that looters cut off the fingers of some of the Café de Paris victims to get their rings. "There were … very nasty people," he is quoted as saying. This is echoed by Alan Kendall in his book, *Their Finest Hour* (1972), who cites the experience of one of the Café de Paris' victims who thought that the hands reaching out to her as she lay covered in debris from the direct hit the café had suffered were trying to help her, only to realise with a shock that the hands were searching for, and stripping off, the rings on her fingers. Thirty people were killed in the bombing of the Café de Paris, including Betty, the daughter of the pre-war Prime Minister Stanley Baldwin.

The Café de Paris was probably a target for blitz or bomb chasers. The chasers were those looters who followed the aircraft into an area as they flew overhead, often having watched for their coming from a nearby hill or high building. They then pounced on an area as it was being bombed or were in the right place to loot it immediately the raiders flew away.

Robbing the Dead

Simon Read mentions the case in London in February 1941 where two rescuers were sentenced to nine and four months' imprisonment respectively for looting a bombed house that was found to contain half a ton of food. The owner of the house had died in the bombing and so had been judged by a higher authority. The presiding magistrate disregarded the provenance of the food and reprimanded the looters for robbing the dead.

Unattended dead bodies were prime targets for looters. Felicity Goodall (*Voices from the Home Front*, 2004) mentions the fact that, in some areas, guards had to be put on holding rooms so that bodies rescued from bombed out buildings were not rifled before being transferred to the mortuary.

Above: Whilst the majority of those in the uniformed services worked diligently in difficult circumstances, some were there solely for the easy access to bombed-out properties full of loot.

Evacuee children brought back to the cities found that there was nothing to do at home, as schools were closed. The result of this was that they were often allowed to run wild, getting into mischief as children will if left to their own devices. Petty thievery sometimes became the order of the day, with bricks stolen from air raid shelters used to shatter windows, break in to empty premises and steal what they could find.

"It's easy ..."

Barbara Nixon was an air raid warden in London. She paints a picture of casual thievery by streetwise children, what she calls 'juvenile swiping', in her autobiography, *Raiders Overhead, A diary of the London blitz*. As she points out, bomb damaged buildings were easy to enter and so removing items of value was a simple operation. When offered a dozen light bulbs for the bargain price of two shillings, Barbara asked if they had come from the company down the street. "Yes, miss, it's easy miss," was the earnest reply from an urchin who went on to explain that they waited until the fire watcher went off to the pub before sneaking inside. The price was then lowered to tenpence. Barbara did not tell her readers whether she was tempted by this offer or not. Later, she records finding a storeroom full of stolen property including blankets, metal boxes, iron bars and saucepans. She strongly suspected that these were spoils looted by a local children's gang.

Meanwhile, Gavin Mortimer reports the Lambeth Juvenile Court proceedings against forty-two child looters. The youngest, aged just seven, had taken money from a gas pre-payment meter. Teenaged girls had helped themselves to the clothes belonging to the dead. Child looters were often the sons and daughters of adult looters and were sent into an area that an adult would find more difficult to target.

Bomb Disposal Looters

Organised looting by servicemen was also encountered. On the front page of *The Nottingham Evening Post* on 28 April 1941, was the tale of a bomb disposal team of thirteen men in Bromley, Kent, who were caught with loot including a clock, a wireless set, a jar of honey and some tea in the back of their van. The lance corporal in charge of the team is reported as confessing, "We are all in it. We take it to the billet and we share."

The Portsmouth Evening News dated 12 March 1941 has a few words regarding the two sailors caught looting wrecked homes following an air raid on the town the night before. The two were caught at 11.15 at night with civilian clothing taken from the premises, including a trilby hat that one of them was wearing.

A different perspective on looting by trusted officials is provided by wartime air raid warden Barbara Nixon, whose colleague was averse to looting domestic premises but was off after pickings the moment a business was hit. This left the rest of his colleagues shorthanded and having to cope as best they could.

These cases demonstrate that looters did not conform to any one stereotype. Rather, they were a cross section of the population, many of whom were, presumably, law-abiding members of society before the temptations of wartime carnage presented them with rich pickings too good to miss.

Looters undoubtedly gave the police more work to do, as they had to patrol bombed areas during the hours of darkness as a deterrent to those up to no good. Roy Ingleton spares a thought for the unfortunate police officers in Oldham, who had to patrol the local cemetery after it had been hit by bombs gone astray from Manchester, just up the road. Reburying dead bodies was not high on anyone's list of priorities and so officers spent unpleasantly eerie nights in the blackout, trying not to step into open graves or walk across decomposing bodies. Hooting owls did not help jangled nerves, either!

Mass Observation

The general public had mixed attitudes to looters. Mass Observation, which recorded the everyday lives and attitudes of people both during and after the war, carried out a survey to determine what the population thought of those who looted. Roy Ingleton recorded some of the findings: 52% of the general public thought looters were 'scum' but 35% were more forgiving, believing that temptation was a great motivator.

Heavy Handed Justice

Justice had to be seen to be done and sentences imposed were supposed to be a deterrent to those who might be tempted by thinking of the spoils to be gained from looting. However, commentators at the time liken the sentences imposed on looters as akin to martial law. *The Yorkshire Post and Leeds Intelligencer,* on 4 March 1941, makes just this point. In a long piece looking at the means and motives of looters, the writer comes to the conclusion that the stiff penalties imposed on those convicted are because, "his offence has been committed under abnormal conditions which render largely inoperative the normal machinery of crime prevention." If word had got around that looting could be got away with, it would have become uncontrollable, hence the heavy sentences imposed on those who were caught.

In November 1940, six Auxiliary Fire Service looters were sentenced to five years' penal servitude at the Old Bailey (National Archives: PREM 4/40/19). They had attended a fire at a public house near to St Paul's cathedral. While they were damping down the fire, their vehicle was searched after clinking glass was heard by police officers. The loot was found in canvas buckets: bottles of whisky, gin and mineral waters, woollen underwear and socks. The firemen had all denied the charge of looting. This case was reported by the *Daily Express* on 23 November 1940, along with three similar cases, that of a labourer who was sentenced to six months' imprisonment for stealing two pairs of lace curtains; another who was sentenced to three weeks for stealing from a bombed flat and a demolition worker who was sentenced to four months' imprisonment for stealing silver spoons and other plate worth £35. These cases came to the Prime Minister's notice. In a minute from the Prime Minister, Winston Churchill, to the Home Secretary, Herbert Morrison, dated 23 November 1940, the disparity in sentencing is highlighted. "Five years penal servitude for stealing whisky for immediate consumption seems out of proportion when compared with sentences of three or six months for stealing valuables." Churchill asks the Home Secretary to review the sentences.

On 7 March 1941, the *Evening Standard* reported the case of two Belgian demolition workers who had been caught stealing. They had pleaded guilty at Clerkenwell Court to charges of looting, stealing a tin of shampoo base from a bombed building and three tankards from a damaged pub, were sentenced to six months' hard labour. The difference between the cases listed was that the six firemen, one of whom had his conviction quashed on appeal, were in a position of trust. They wore the uniform of the emergency services and should have been above the temptations offered by unprotected wares lying about after a catastrophic event. The reality though, was that those fighting to keep Britain going on the home front night after night, and who had been completely trustworthy before the war, were as imperfect as any other person, particularly as war time rationing was biting.

On 3 June 1941, the Home Secretary sent the Prime Minister a minute detailing the number of looters and the length of sentence handed out to looters up until that point in the war.

Length of Sentence	Number of persons sentenced
Five years and over	24
One year but less than five years	67
Six months but less than one year	82
Under six months	116

Twenty-five people were fined, with fines ranging from £1 to £15. There were also cases of persons being bound over to keep the peace or sent to approved schools but the numbers for these were not itemised in the minute.

The Home Secretary was aware of the disparity of sentencing but, as he pointed out to the Prime Minister, he had reservations about interfering in the due process of the law. In a letter dated 20 May 1941, he says:

'I remain of the opinion that it would not be wise to interfere with such sentences at the present time. While it is true that looting does not seem to be greatly on the increase at present, it is still far too prevalent, and may well become worse at any moment with the intensification of bombing. The present cases could not be dealt with apart from a number of others, and in any event we cannot, in my opinion, afford to give any impression that the Government take a more lenient view of looting than the Courts.'

He did, however, eventually review earlier severe sentencing and those with a previous good character were released on licence if they had served half of their time in jail.

People from all walks of life were tempted to loot, some from thoughtlessness and others from greed. Wartime conditions, unusual but immediate, brought with it temptations that blemished the hitherto spotless reputations of those who, in 'normal' life would have been shocked by such behaviour. Sadly, World War Two brought out the worst in many.

Above: Britain imported 55 million tonnes of food a year before the war. It was vital to keep as much food coming into the country as possible throughout.

> The government, worried about rising
> food prices leaving poorer families
> struggling.... decided that the only fair
> way to manage increasingly meagre
> supplies was to introduce rationing.

2
The Black Market

The Concise Oxford Dictionary defines '**black market**' as:
Noun – an illicit traffic in officially controlled or scarce commodities.
A 'black marketeer' is defined as:
Noun – a person who engages in a black market.

Britain was at war again. The realities of life on the home front as the
fighting dragged on were harsh. Total effort was put into supplying those
fighting for King and Country. This meant that there was little left for those
at home and what there was had to be stretched to benefit all. Britain, an
island nation, was largely dependent on supplies coming from abroad to fill
its larders with food. Before the war, Britain imported 55 million tonnes of
foodstuff a year from countries all over the world, mostly by sea. With the
outbreak of war, the importation of food had to be curbed, either because
of the dangers of transporting it, or because of the lack of transport vessels
due to the sheer number of ships destroyed by the enemy. Convoys were
hunted and targeted by enemy submarine patrols. By 1941, ships were
being sunk at a rate of three a day (Hodge, 2012). At the end of the war
1,315 British merchant ships had been sunk by U-Boat action
(www.USMM.org) and, unsurprisingly, this impacted severely on the variety
of fare available to the housewife. The government, worried about rising
food prices leaving poorer families struggling, and the effects on the masses
of food hoarding by the few, decided that the only fair way to manage the
even distribution of the increasingly meagre supplies coming ashore, was to
introduce rationing.

This began on 8 January 1940 and was to drag on for fourteen years.
Britain's population had to get used to hardship and lack of choice at a time
when, ironically, many were better off financially than they had ever been
due to increased employment for the war effort. Rationing finally ceased on
4 July 1954, by which time it was utterly detested.

Above: Shopkeepers had to tot up points and cut out coupons so that the housewife would buy the correct entitlement to rationed goods.

Ration books were issued for all and they were to be used at designated retailers. In the days before the supermarket, different commodities were available in different shops. Hence, the average housewife found herself queuing at the grocer for vegetables and other items, the butcher for meat, the baker for bread and so on. Shopping, in an era before the refrigerator that meant that most housewives shopped daily, became a time-consuming business as shopkeepers totted up points and crossed through sections on the ration cards for each member of the family to ensure that the correct ration was allocated. Bacon, butter and sugar were the first foods to be rationed. These were soon followed by meat in March 1940, cooking fat and tea in July 1940, jam in March 1941, cheese in May 1941 and eggs in June 1941. By the end of the war in 1945, the list included tinned tomatoes, rice,

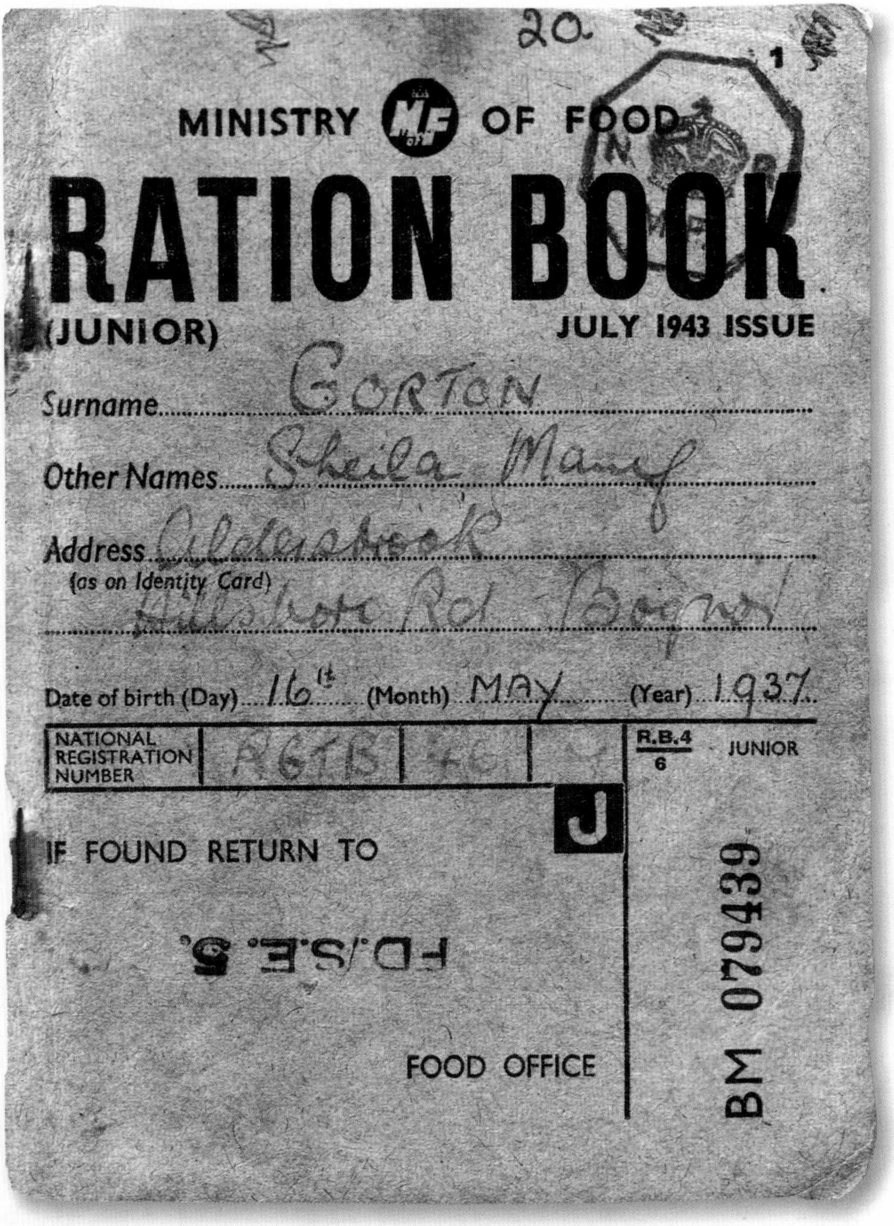

MINISTRY **MF** OF FOOD

RATION BOOK

(JUNIOR)   **JULY 1943 ISSUE**

Surname...... *GORTON*

Other Names...... *Sheila Mary*

Address...... *Aldershook*
(as on Identity Card)
...... *Hillside Rd Bognor*

Date of birth (Day) *16th* (Month) *MAY* (Year) *1937*

| NATIONAL REGISTRATION NUMBER | *AGTB* *461* | R.B.4 6 | JUNIOR |

J

IF FOUND RETURN TO

FD./S.E. 5.

FOOD OFFICE

BM 079439

Above: Rationing finally ceased in 1954, by which time it was thoroughly detested.

peas, canned fruit, biscuits, breakfast cereals, milk and dried fruit, reflecting the increasing devastation being inflicted on the merchant fleet. Potatoes and fresh fruit were not rationed but the scarcity of apples, for example, made the newspapers (*Liverpool Daily Post*, 30 August 1944).

With the war came hardship

Rations were distributed by weight, monetary value or points. One person's typical weekly allowance would be: one fresh egg; 4oz (100g) margarine and bacon/ham (about four rashers); 2oz (50g) butter and tea; 1oz (25g) cheese; 3 pints (1800ml) of fresh milk (depending on availability) and 8oz (225g) sugar. Meat was allocated by price to the value of 1s 2d, so cheaper cuts became popular. In addition, a packet of dried eggs and 12oz (350g) of sweets (the ration was halved in 1946) were available every four weeks and 1lb (450g) of jam every two months. Each person also had sixteen points each week that could be used on any item they wished or could be pooled or saved to buy pulses, cereals, tinned goods, dried fruit, biscuits and jam. Bread, not limited during the war itself, was added to the ration just after the hostilities ended, in 1946.

American servicemen in Britain, used to ample rations and uncaring of waste, were urged to 'go easy' if invited to a British home for a meal. 'It might be the family's rations for a whole week spread out to show their hospitality.' (*Welcome to Britain*)

All over Britain, people were urged to 'Dig for Victory' as playing fields and gardens were ploughed up and used to grow vegetables. The keeping of rabbits, chickens or pigs increased, as they were reared to supplement

Above: A week's food ration. American servicemen were cautioned to 'go easy' as hospitality spread over a table could be the entire family's ration for a week.

Above: Playing fields and gardens were ploughed up and used to grow much needed vegetables to supplement the nation's increasingly meagre rations.

Above: Allotments sprang up on every available piece of ground, whether it be garden or park. People from all walks of life were encouraged to grow vegetables.

the meagre meat ration. Mushrooms were advertised as a 'War Food Crop' by the British Mushroom Industry in national newspapers and readers were urged to grow them all year round, with the promise that their crops would be bought from them at a guaranteed price, as part of the war effort.

In addition to the rationing of food, other items were added to the list. Petrol was rationed soon after the war began in 1939. The beginning of June 1941 saw the start of clothes rationing, which continued until March 1949. The next month saw the beginning of coal rationing. This was not a scarce commodity. The problem was that there were not enough men to mine it as the call up of experienced miners took its toll. *The Daily Express* on Saturday May 13 1944 carries a report on Bevin Boys, young men called up to work in the mines between 1943 and 1948. They were nicknamed after Ernest Bevin, the Minister for Labour and National Service who instituted the policy of placing one man in every ten men called up in a coal mine rather than the armed forces. This was deeply unpopular as the work done by the Bevin Boys was largely unrecognised. Bevin Boys wore no uniform and were often mistaken for draft dodgers. The work was also dangerous. *The Daily Telegraph and Morning Post*, on Wednesday May 2 1945, reported mining accident figures given by the Ministry of Fuel and Power: 1942: 946; 1943: 778; 1944: 674. The country could not afford to be squeamish and those who refused to work in the mines were dealt with harshly. William Houlihan in Greenwich and Robert William Olive, in West London, both aged 18, were sentenced to six weeks in jail for refusing to work in the mines. Houlihan stated that he had wanted to go to sea. In Dartford, Kent, Charles Walter Young was fined £10 after he stated that he 'could not stick coalmining.'

Gas and electricity soon joined coal as all fuels were rationed by the middle of 1942. One item that was sorely missed was soap. This went on ration in February 1942. The friendly American narrator in *Welcome to Britain* comments, 'One of the things the English always had enough of in the past was soap. Now it is so scarce that girls working in the factories often cannot get the grease off their hands or out of their hair.' The oil in soap was the magic ingredient as it was edible and so used in food production. Toilet paper was scarce by 1944, while handkerchiefs were 'priceless' according to Felicity Goodall, commenting in *Voices from the Home Front* (2004).

With the imposition of the blackout, huge quantities of black material were produced but little clothing material. A culture of make do and mend soon grew up as the clothing coupons supplied on the ration were sufficient to buy only one new set of clothes a year. The ration of adult coupons was initially sixty coupons, but was later reduced to forty-eight. Children had ten more. This seemingly ample supply of

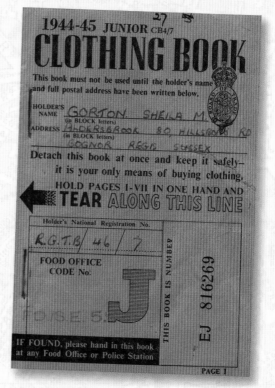

Above: A child's clothing coupon book. Children were allowed ten more coupons than adults. Even so, many could not afford to buy new clothes and often children found themselves in hand-me-downs.

coupons seems sparse when looking at the number of coupons needed for what we, in twenty-first century peace time, take for granted. A pair of men's shoes was seven coupons. A boy's pair was three. A pair of men's trousers was eight coupons. Shorts for a boy were three. A lady's woollen dress was eleven coupons and a pair of stockings were two coupons. A girl's blouse was three coupons. It is easy to see why gravy browning became popular to paint a simulated seam up the back of a woman's legs if she ran out of coupons to buy more stockings. Stockings were always in demand on the black market and were often the one item that was most missed by women during the war. Lisle stockings, dense and knitted from cotton, were the unpopular alternative. Many women wore short socks instead.

The clothing coupon system caused problems for mothers with growing children, who outgrew their clothes quickly, despite the extra ten coupons to compensate. The fact that prices increased with scarcity did not help, either (Marsh, 2014). Children got used to wearing patched hand-me-downs to make sure that the very last bit of wear was obtained before they were recycled as dusters or cut up to make something else. Indeed, both adults and children often looked as tatty as the unpainted buildings and unkept gardens in the streets, particularly if being bombed out was added to the mix. James Marsh was a child during the Second World War. He remembers:

> There would be a knock on our front door and one of the mothers of the older boys in the road would be standing on our front step. "Oh, hello, Mrs Marsh," she would say, "my David has grown out of these trousers but there's plenty of wear in them yet. I'm sure they'll fit your little Jimmy a treat." Then 'little Jimmy' would be sent upstairs to try them on, coming back down to be subjected to close scrutiny … "Oh yes," they would both chorus, "they fit him a treat." (Legg and Marsh, 2013)

Of course, in such circumstances, if a thing is scarce it creates want. Until 1941, when the Ministry of Food stepped in and introduced price controls, retailers were able to make excessive profits from increasingly scarce items. A thriving black market grew up with those who could obtain unavailable goods profiteering from demand for items in short supply. There were few individuals who would not buy something they missed if it was offered to them for sale, ration books not needed, no questions asked. The black market did much to narrow class divides as people from all walks of life bought items offered by black marketeers eager to exploit all the opportunities that wartime rules and regulations opened. Dishonest and anti-social practices abounded: milk was watered down to make it go further (*East Grinstead Observer*, 16th September, 1944); so-called milk substitutes were found to be mixtures of flour, salt and baking powder (Angus Calder,

The People's War, 1969) and some butchers demanded a tip to supply meat (Jonathan Croall, *Don't You Know There's A War On*, 1989). Nevertheless, the resulting booty was eagerly bought by those who had a higher disposable income than ever before now that they were conscripted into the forces or toiling in the factories.

Items available

Although many were outraged at the antics of those widely regarded as parasites, others shrugged their shoulders at the war shortages they faced and did whatever they had to do to provide for their family. Thus, if you had the money, whatever you wanted was available and someone usually knew the right person to go to, despite the best efforts of the Board of Trade and the Ministry of Food, whose inspectors, numbering nearly a thousand, policed black market activity. The theft of thousands of ration books, worth half a million pounds on the black market, from a cellar closely guarded by security officers, was unreported by the media because of the damage it would do to public confidence in the system. Sometimes though it was a case of being in the right place at the right time, as Ingleton notes when he mentions the case of the senior police officer in the West Midlands Police who received a bottle of whiskey in appreciation of the actions of one of his subordinates (who had virtuously declined it) and promptly took it around to the local pub and sold it to the landlord.

Philip MacDougall mentions the gang of servicemen at Tangmere airfield, a short distance from Chichester in Sussex (*Chichester: Murders & Misdemeanours*, 2009). These enterprising individuals stole over 700 gallons of fuel from the airfield in a six-month period in 1941 and sold it on to a range of purchasers. Seven of the nine members of the gang were fined and the remaining two were sentenced to hard labour at the Police Court in Chichester in August 1941.

The Daily Express (13 May 1944) carries the story of the British Forces Gift Shop in Naples, run by the NAAFI, which sold stockings at 10s a pair to forces personnel. Mrs D Erith, of Whitecross Avenue, Bristol was sent a pair by her soldier husband, with a receipt and a letter asking what she thought of them as they were so expensive. No doubt thrilled to be the recipient of such a prize without having to use precious tokens, she was dismayed to find that they were not quite as they seemed. She took them to be examined by 'an expert' who pronounced them to be the 'cheapest rayon I have ever seen' and worth 1/6d at the most. A NAAFI official stated that the stockings were not on the list of items sold officially to the forces through the shop and speculated that they might have been bought privately and used to stock the shop. Prices for all items sold in the shop were set according to local valuation. An investigation was underway.

Gangster 'Mad' Frankie Fraser (1923 - 2014) mentions Bobby Hedley in his book *Mad Frank and Friends*. Hedley was known as 'Silver' because of the frequency with which he robbed Silvers, the tailors in Tower Bridge Road, London. With clothing rationed, suit cloth was a valuable commodity and brought a good price on the black market when sold on to other tailors.

How were black market goods obtained?

It is no coincidence that incidents of theft went up during the war. Houses left empty by owners evacuated from the city meant unattended and unguarded property just waiting for house breakers to pick through. Homes,

Above: Supplies that did make it past the U-boats were unloaded at the docks, giving ample opportunity to thieves waiting to pounce.

shops and offices that had been bombed resulted in their contents lying in the open for prying eyes and sly fingers to find. What harm would there be in taking some of these? After all, the insurance would pay out …

The public, tired and fed up with war, were sometimes less vigilant than they should have been when in public places, such as air raid shelters. The London Underground, teeming with blitz-weary Londoners, was also rife with pickpockets.

In the early hours of the morning of 11 May 1941, 58 Old Compton Street, the premises of a bedding manufacturer, was set ablaze during the longest and most profound night of bombing of the London Blitz. Fire crews were called but their capacity was stretched beyond breaking point as they were also battling to save Westminster Palace, hit and with fire raging. As it became obvious that the factory premises were going to burn down and that the fire was spreading rapidly to neighbouring businesses, police ordered that Old Compton Street be evacuated and that as much stock as possible be removed from the shops and stacked in the street outside. Gavin Mortimer reports that within minutes 'a sordid gaggle of spivs and chancers' was haggling with the shop keepers for the best price for the salvaged goods.

The Daily Herald (15 April 1941) reported that farmers in Kent were patrolling their farms with shot guns after a spate of sheep were killed in the fields and bundled into cars to be sold as meat on the black market. The Home Guard had been alerted to keep an eye open for the so-called 'Butcher Gangs.'

In the meantime, the same newspaper reported convoys of lorries loaded with supplies from a depot town and destined for a blitzed city, which arrived incomplete, some lorries having been high-jacked on the journey.

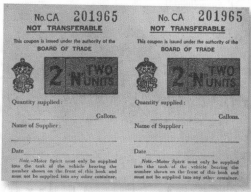

Above: Petrol coupon issued by the Board of Trade

The *Derby Daily Telegraph* (3 July 1945) reports the theft of 12,000 petrol coupons, the equivalent of 'hundreds of thousands of gallons' of fuel, from the Clifton, Bristol offices of the Ministry for Transport. The coupons were in low denominations, from one to five gallons, and were designated as being for heavy goods vehicles. The theft was clearly carefully planned as nothing else was taken. That so many were stolen points to the demand for coupons for resale on the lucrative black market or for use by those engaged in moving illicit goods. That the report of the theft of such a large quantity of petrol coupons was to be found on page 8 of a provincial newspaper is significant. The theft was reported where similar thefts earlier in the war were not made known to the public for fear of affecting the morale of a beleaguered populace and shaking their faith in the system. However, by giving the crime just a few short lines on an obscure page, the reporting obligation of the press was satisfied without undue attention being drawn to the crime itself, or those who were involved in it, thus giving the police more opportunity to find the culprits and keeping the status quo with the public.

Raynes Minns (*Bombers and Mash*, 1980) notes that huge amounts of merchandise were stolen from the railways during the war years. In 1941, eye-boggling figures for the period are mentioned: £500,000 from the London, Midland & Scottish (LMS), £200,000 from the Great Western Railway (GWR), £160,000 from the Southern Railway. As the regular railway staff had largely been called up, temporary staff were frequently blamed for the thefts, or any of the many army deserters drifting through the country, looking for any means they could find to make a living while on the run.

Meanwhile, in Walsall, Brenda Lane, a twenty-one-year-old shop assistant, was fined £2 by magistrates for buying clothes coupons offered to her by a child when they were in a shop in Park Street in the town. Lane paid 11s 6d for the eleven and a half coupons. The *Evening Despatch* (Friday 30 June 1944) reports that a Board of Trade official had commented that children had realised that the coupons were worth money and sold them accordingly.

The Recorder of Liverpool, Mr E G Hemmerde, commented in 1942 that the theft of food from the Liverpool Docks and elsewhere was nothing short of a national scandal. He wondered if it was the work of the Fifth Column, out to sabotage the country. The *Daily Record* on 12 January 1942, which reported Mr Hemmerde's comments, noted that the scale of thefts of vital supplies was on a 'scale … never known before.' It gave as an example the theft of 40,000 servicewomen's undergarments, which had had to be written off as they had been missing for so long. The newspaper opined that the thefts were to order and were costing the country many hundreds of thousands of pounds.

Who was involved in the Black Market?

Was the Black Marketeer the loveable spiv from the television sitcom *Dad's Army*; a figure of fun such as 'Flash Harry' from the films about the raucous school for girls, St Trinians or a more sinister person? Roy Ingleton, in his interesting and highly readable look at the ever-increasing role of the police at this time, *The Gentlemen at War, Policing Britain 1939 – 1945*, offers this

Above: 1942, a black marketeer selling cigarettes to office staff. If you had the money, you could obtain just about anything on the Black Market.

description of the, usually, 'one man concern, the "spiv"': 'Often a deserter from the services or a draft dodger, living on his wits, this type of petty criminal was more often a receiver than an active thief, a retailer rather than a wholesaler or supplier.' As Raynes Minns puts it, the spiv represented a 'flashy flaunting' of regulations, dressed in his distinctive trilby hat, sharp suit and colourful shoes.

The Local Blackmarketeer

James Marsh was born in 1940 in Southampton. He has written about his wartime childhood and the life he led growing up after the war. He has vivid memories of the local black market trader.

'The Black Marketeer I knew personally was Mr Fryer. He had a house opposite us in Belgrave Road and every time we were sent to him it was a frightening experience to us children. He was a surly man. His front door was never locked. You went in and into the front room. He had a board across the whole room. We would shout "Shop!" and he would come shuffling out of the back room, demanding to know what we wanted. We would just hand the bag to him and say, "Mummy would like this." He didn't like children and we didn't like him but the most important thing was he knew every one of us – he knew who we were. Therefore, he knew who Mummy was. In the bag was a list and the money was inside it. We never had to take the ration books when we shopped with Mr Fryer. To go anywhere else, you had to be registered with the shops but not with him you didn't.

'The things that were on the list were things that were in short supply: butter, sugar, cooking fat – you couldn't get it. Milk. You couldn't get fresh milk. We had powdered milk. He didn't. He had fresh. If you wanted it, you went to him. We didn't know where he got it all from. That was his secret. All we knew was that we had to hand the bag over to him and when it came back over the counter there were a lot of things in there. We ran out as fast as we could, back to Mummy. At one time or another, we were all sent to him. [James was one of four children in the family during the war.] He was very much the Black Marketeer.

'I never saw clothing. It was likely he had this but my mother only bought groceries from him. The room had a board across it to make a counter and then the rest of the room was blocked off. Mr Fryer used to disappear from view behind the counter and you would hear rustling noises and then he would come and plonk the bag down. We never saw under the counter, what he had or didn't have. He never said at any time, "I haven't got that. Tell your mum I haven't got that." He never ever said that.

'The whole street went to Mr Fryer. We never saw the goods arrive. There were back cut-ways behind the house and the goods would come in through the back door into the house. He got away with it. He had virtually an open shop yet he got away with it. He would only serve people he knew though. If anyone just turned up, he would say, "What do you want? I don't do that, go away." It could have been a lady policeman.'

Black marketeers did not just operate in Britain. Men sometimes deserted the Armed Forces purely for financial gain, willing to risk stiff prison sentences or worse in order to steal rations and equipment destined for troops on the front line. As Charles Glass (2013) points out, Allied deserters wrought havoc with their plundering, sometimes at gunpoint, to supply the black markets of Rome, Paris and Naples between 1944 and 1946. As a result, for example, General Patton's tanks were short of fuel and men at the front faced potentially life-threatening shortages of food, blankets and ammunition.

American-Italian gangster Vito Genovese, on the run from America after allegedly shooting mobster Ferdinand Boccia in 1934, prospered in war-torn Italy as a Mafia boss, ingratiating himself with Benito Mussolini's son-in-law, Gian Gelleazzo Ciano, Count of Cortellazzo and Buccari, Italy's Foreign Minister in 1936. Genovese ran a huge Black Market racket in Naples. When the Allied Forces arrived in Italy in 1943, Genovese quickly changed sides, becoming a trusted aide at the US Army headquarters in Naples, where his language skills were useful. However, unbeknown to his new employers, his black market operations continued as he stole army trucks and foodstuffs, often transported in lorries driven by deserters. He was arrested in 1944 when the American Military Police investigated the Black Market operation. It was then that information came forward about the Boccia murder and the American arrest warrant was revealed. Sent back to the United States for trial, all of the witnesses met untimely deaths and, with no evidence to convict him, he was a free man. Genovese was to end his days in 1969, ten years into a fifteen-year jail term for importing and selling heroin.

Above: Vito Genovese, Black Market gangster.

In France, American deserters presented a new battlefront to cope with when they high-jacked Army lorries at gunpoint and fought battles with the Military Police bent on stopping their illicit aspirations.

Organised Crime

Black market goods were, inevitably, the honey to which organised crime was drawn. The theft of ration books on such a scale mentioned earlier was hardly a crime that could be accomplished by one person acting by himself. As Paul Lund notes, '… World War II (1939 – 1945) provided the greatest single opportunity – the black market – for the underworld …' (*Organised Crime*, 2004).

The Sabini Brothers

The long reign of the Irish/Italian Sabini Brothers, from Holborn in London, with their extortion rackets at race courses, robberies and gambling palaces, was crumbling due to jealous rivalries with other gangs by the beginning of the war and was brought to an end in 1940, when they were interned as enemy aliens after Italy sided with the enemy. Headed by Charles 'Darby' Sabini (born Ottavio Handley in 1888 and christened Ollovia Sabini, the illegitimate son of an Italian immigrant, Ottavio Sabini, and Eliza Handley), the Sabini Brothers were the nearest thing Britain had to the organised Mafia crime families in the United States. However, where the Mafia were widespread and widely feared, the Sabini gang were active in only the south of England in the inter-war period and were based in the Italian enclaves of Clerkenwell, East London. The brothers, Darby, Fred and Charles, were chiefly engaged in theft, extortion and illegal gambling, although territorial conflicts with other gangs were also common. Edward Greeno was a Scotland Yard police officer who investigated a number of high profile cases. He reports tit-for-tat beatings between members of the Sabini gang and the Birmingham boys in Islington in the 1920s (*War on the Underworld*, 1960). Darby was the self-styled 'King of the Race Track Gangs,' mainly at Epsom, Brighton and Lewes. Providing 'protection' for the illegal bookmakers at race tracks, whose pockets bulged with cash, was a lucrative part of their business. Edward Greeno notes that Sabini and his 'thugs' intimidated their victims by standing sideways-on so that the bookmakers could see the hammers in their pockets. It is rumoured that on Epsom Derby Day, the gang could make £20,000 from the bookmakers by extortion. The gang was reportedly three hundred strong and members were known for their willingness to use a razor blade in attacks, although Darby himself, as with most bullies, was squeamish about using such a weapon and would send others to do the dirty work. Assault charges were common but witnesses were, unsurprisingly, slow in coming forward. 'It was ever thus,' commented Greeno. The Sabini Brothers forged powerful connections with police to try to keep other gangs out of their business, and with politicians and judges, but rival gangs were ever pushing to take over, in particular, the Birmingham Boys, the Yiddishers, the Cortesi family and the White family. The Second World War was disastrous for the Sabini gang, with its connections to Jewish bookmakers and its Italian roots. Darby Sabini was arrested in April 1940

> **Sabini and his 'thugs' intimidated their victims by standing sideways-on so that the bookmakers could see the hammers in their pockets.**

at the greyhound stadium in Hove. He was interned as an enemy alien for a year. After this, the lure of the black market called and he was to serve three years in jail for receiving stolen goods. After the war, the gang was taken over by the White Family and Darby slipped into obscurity working as a bookmaker. He died in 1950.

Diamonds are forever …

The biggest name in a black market racket frequently managed to get off the hook when confronted by the police.

Diamonds, other precious gems and jewellery were all the more precious during wartime. The Gem Diamonds (Control of Manufacture) Order, 1942 made it a Board of Trade offense to manufacture gem diamonds. The National Archives' files on the alleged diamond black marketeers Bialogora and Saperstein, dated 1943, make interesting reading (MEPO 3/2340). In his statement to the police, Chiel Bialogora, a 22-year-old diamond polisher who was resident in Birmingham and worked for Mssers Diamond Tools Ltd in that city, was approached by Belgian refugee Eisa Saperstein in London. Saperstein asked Bialogora if he would polish 'brute' diamonds, what the trade called 'raw' or unpolished stones. A payment of £68 was agreed upon for the first three. Further stones were forthcoming, all of which Bialogora had polished at his company's premises. He returned ten polished stones to Sapperstein and still had ten in his possession, valued at £250, along with a valuable diamond ring, when he was stopped by police.

According to Saperstein's statement made on 9 February 1943, he had been a diamond dealer in Antwerp. He came to the UK in June 1940 with his wife and son as a refugee. He was granted a Home Office permit to establish himself as a diamond dealer or broker for a period of twelve months on 1 December 1942. He did not declare the 200 separate stones he took with him from Belgium, roughly 130 carats of rough or 'Brute' diamonds, when he arrived in Liverpool as he was not asked about them. He knew Bialogora's father as a trustworthy man and had faith in his son, who he knew was a diamond merchant. He gave twenty diamonds to Bialogora saying that he could buy them himself or sell them on commission. He asked for £120 for the lot. He also gave Bialogora his wife's single stone ring, valued at about £165, which Bialogora promised to sell on commission.

Bialogora later returned ten stones saying that they were 'no good to him' but kept the other ten and Saperstein's wife's ring. Saperstein asserted that Bialogora did not tell him what he was going to do with the ten stones he kept but he did not receive payment for them. He did not see Bialogora again and heard about his arrest from a third party, a diamond dealer in Hatton Garden, Mr Weiner, whom Saperstein met on 7 February 1943.

Saperstein denied asking Bialogora to polish the diamonds. He was able to identify only two of the diamonds confiscated from Bialogora as they had been polished. He did, however, identify the ring found on Saperstein as being his wife's. He asserted that he was not aware that it was an offence to sell his own personal brute diamonds without proper authority. Convinced that Saperstein was lying but unable to prove it, the authorities could not proceed with a prosecution against him.

Bialogora, along with his accomplices, Dutchman Elias Zomerplaag, George Alfons Meaking and Albert Fray, who had all actually polished the stones, were charged by the Board of Trade under the Gem Diamonds (Control of Manufacture) Order, 1942 with the unlawful manufacture of gem diamonds between 1 January and 16 February 1943. The four appeared before the Stipendiary Magistrate at the Victoria Law Courts, Birmingham, on 17 March 1943. Bialogora was charged with aiding and abetting each of the other three defendants in the commission of the offence. All pleaded guilty. Bialogora was fined £20 on each summons and ordered to pay £1 1s 0d costs. The rest were ordered to pay £25 with £1 1s 0d costs. Saperstein got away with the black market crime, but did have the diamonds found in Bialogora's possession confiscated.

How were those involved in the Black Market seen by the authorities?

The authorities took a dim view of those involved in the Black Market.

One problem was the lack of willingness to report infringements or those involved. Racketeering was rife but such was the hold on the legitimate trader that few were willing to report abuses. It was everyone's duty to report evidence of racketeering and then to follow through with an appearance in court, of course. The gulf between where duty lay and the reality of life was usually where prosecutions came unstuck. *The Daily Herald*, (17 April 1941) reported a case where a large company had been charged £80 for eggs they had not received. They refused to pay what amounted to toll money and then found themselves boycotted, with no eggs being supplied at all. They reported the situation but would not go to court as they felt that to do so would lead to their being victimised later.

The Ministry of Food employed enforcement officers, usually former CID police officers, but it was an uphill struggle. There was endless variety in the ways and means that blackmarketeers could find to cheat the system, including a loop-hole in price legislation that meant that some wholesalers were evading the maximum price control set by the Ministry of Food by sending their produce direct to retailers and having payment made directly to Eire. They would then be given a rake-off from the profits.

Rationing, by its very nature, was supposed to offer equality of opportunity to all. Black Marketeering undermined that equality. When John Whyley Stanley (31) and Jospeh Linden Bant (40) were charged with stealing two tonnes of butter on 1 July 1941 by the Birmingham City Police, and Reuben Charles Haden (32) and William Fairburn were found to have received it, there was no mercy. Mr Justice Stable, at the Birmingham Assizes, sentenced them each to three years' penal servitude. A fifth man, Percy Jeavons, a dental mechanic, was found guilty of conspiracy to steal and given twenty-one days in jail (*Hull Daily Mail*, 21 July 1941). Most of the newspaper coverage of the crime headlined the men as 'Racketeers.' To put the seriousness of what, at first glance, may seem a trivial offence into context, two tonnes of butter represented 35,000 two-ounce rations, or, to put it another way, these would be the rations for one person for 700 years. The butter had been stolen by van from the Lightfoot Refrigeration Company on 6 June and then traced to the five men (*Gloucester Echo*, 20 June 1941). The robbery was described by Mr Justice Stable as 'deliberately planned' against the country he described as a 'besieged fortress,' (*Nottingham Evening Post*, 21 July 1941).

The theft of more than nine tons of sugar from Tate & Lyle in Liverpool by three trusted employees who had each worked at the firm for more than twenty years was dealt with sternly. Alec Baskott, the warehouse foreman, John Crighton, the warehouse chargehand, and leading stower Thomas Sutton, all from Liverpool, were each sentenced to three years' penal servitude for the theft. Their accomplice, who sold the sugar and was said to be the brains of the outfit, David Johnstone Gray, an engineer

It is undoubtedly true that for many the black market was a way of life, offering either a chance of wealth to the unscrupulous or the opportunity to escape the harsh realities of rationing to the desperate. The nature of man is to exploit situations and this is precisely what happened during the war years.

from Blackpool, was sentenced to penal servitude for four years. The stolen sugar found its way to a Blackpool creamery and was made into ice cream. The creamery's manager, Alfred William Gosling, and ice cream maker James Henry Sanderson, were each found guilty of receiving stolen goods. Their defence, and that of Gray, was that they knew the transaction was for black market goods, but they had not realised the sugar was stolen. Gosling served 15 months in jail and Sanderson 12 months. (*Dundee Courier*, 14 November 1946).

To hinder bombers, whose pilots would use any available light to guide them... a complete blackout was ordered. It came into force on 1 September, two days before the start of the war.

3

Crimes by Blackout

The Concise Oxford Dictionary defines '**blackout**' in this context as: **Noun** – a compulsory period of darkness as a precaution against air raids.

The whole country observed the blackout, designed to limit the amount of light available to guide enemy aircraft on bombing raids. Darkness came swiftly to Britain. Whilst the hopeful were still keeping their fingers crossed that the country would not go to war, the government was busily preparing for the inevitable. The Emergency Powers Defence Act (passed on 24 August 1939) brought in a raft of new regulations and the subsequent Emergency Powers Act, consolidating some of the first act's rules, was passed on 22 May 1940. The Air Ministry had predicted enemy night bombing raids, with much civilian loss of life and damage to buildings as a consequence. To hinder the bombers, whose pilots would use any available light to guide them to the mission objective, a complete blackout was ordered. It came into force on 1 September, two days before the start of the war. From then onwards, not one chink of light was allowed to show from any window. Copious amounts of cheap black cloth were produced so that all sections of the community could afford to adhere to the new regulations.Britain's civilians then had the onerous daily task of putting up and taking down the curtaining. For some, this was to prove difficult as they had to devise ways and means to black out windows in stone walls, where simply sticking the material across the window would not do. In addition to blacking out windows, car headlights had to be masked, streetlights were turned off, torches were covered and any miscellaneous lighting, such as, for example, the tiny glow from cigarette ends, was banned. The whole

Left: The whole country observed the blackout, designed to limit the amount of light available to guide enemy aircraft on bombing raids.

country was literally plunged into darkness every evening. Blackout timings were displayed every day by Air Raid Precautions (ARP) wardens and these timings were also printed in local newspapers, along with the moon's rising and setting times, which information was suddenly useful. To help decrease the rising number of accidents in the streets, white lines were painted in the middle of the road and the kerbs were painted white so that any drivers who plucked up the courage to negotiate the highways in the darkness would have a guide along the way.

It was now an offence to let any light appear through the gloom of the blackout, with the threat of, at the very least, a stiff telling off from an ARP warden, or, for repeat offenders, a trip to court, where unfriendly magistrates handed out hefty fines to transgressors.

Local newspapers are very revealing in opening up the everyday world on the home front during this time. *The Sussex Express and County Herald* (Hailsham and Heathfield Edition) for Friday 27 November 1942, carries 'News From the Villages'. It reported the case of Mrs Yvonne Best, who pleaded guilty to 'permitting a light to be displayed' at her home, The Grove, in Mayfield, on 12 October and again on 2 November. The house stood close to the main road and had three windows with no blackout curtains at all and another with what was described as 'white material' across it. It was further

It was now an offence to let any light appear through the gloom of the blackout

reported that there was a two-inch gap of light at the base of the front door. Mrs Best had been similarly prosecuted a year before, on 14 October, when she was fined £3, with 4s costs. Now up before the magistrate once more, she tried to explain herself by stating that the house had thirty windows and she had five children to look after. 'It was a scramble each night' to get the blackout in place in time. She was given short shrift as the chairman of the bench remarked that, 'he could not help that!' Mrs Best was fined £5 and 4s costs for each offence. A further charge, for 8 November, was not taken forward as she had since put in place adequate black out curtaining. Mrs Best was no doubt left smarting from the large fine, £10 being a sizeable amount at the time, and from the indignity of repeated court appearances. Mrs Best was not alone. By the end of the war, there had been 114,000 prosecutions for black out offences.

As Simon Read succinctly puts it, 'London's new dark age was a breeding ground of mischief and crooked activity,' (*The Blackout Murders*, 2006). Apart from criminalising the usually law-abiding population, the blackout was a boon to opportunist thieves. The *Lancashire Evening Post* of 3 August 1940 carries the story of looter John Smith, a forty-one-year-old private in the Pioneer Corps. A 'Northern Police Court' sentenced him to fourteen

Above: Advertisement for blackout curtaining, *Aldershot News*, 25 October 1940.

days' imprisonment for using the blackout to steal a woman's suitcase from a train. When the air raid siren sounded, the woman put her case on the luggage rack in the first class compartment and then left the train to go to the air raid shelter. Smith, from Glasgow, who was in uniform at the time, was seen rifling through the case's contents having cut the bag open.

In the meantime, Frank Forster, speaking in Felicity Goodall's *Voices from the Home Front*, lived in Chester and was concerned about his fiancée making her way home safely through the black out for a very different reason - troops were filling the city and drunkenness was rife.

The complete darkness also offered cover for more serious crime, from prostitution to murder.

Prostitution

The blackout was a heaven-sent opportunity for prostitution. The streets were cloaked in darkness so pitch that newspapers printed the phases of the moon and the time it rose, as the more moonlight there was, the fewer accidents happened. Shadowy street corners, dark alleys and gloomy doorways all provided a working environment for hookers out on the street touting for business. In London, Hyde Park was a favourite haunt and a whistle would guide a punter to a warm welcome amongst the bushes. Prostitution, by its very nature, is a dangerous business and the home front during this period offered more challenges than usual to streetwalkers, who had to contend with the darkness of the blackout and bombing raids at night, a prime time for their business, as well as the usual pitfalls of disease or violence from their customers. There were plenty of punters, too. Wave upon wave of servicemen, either British or from overseas, were eager to pay for what they missed by being away from home.

> **Shadowy street corners, dark alleys and gloomy doorways all provided a working environment for hookers out on the street touting for business.**

Prostitution during the period was regarded as sordid and of little interest to British organised crime. Until the beginning of the war, organised prostitution was the preserve of French gangs. A series of murders of prostitutes during the latter part of the 1930s was rumoured to have been the work of the Messina Brothers seeking to break the stranglehold the French had on the trade. In 1936, in Soho, Constance Smith was found strangled with a length of copper insulated wire and had been battered about the head with a flat iron. The later murders of two more alleged prostitutes and a pimp were linked with that of Smith by the press.

Donald Thomas speculated that these were murders 'to set an example' but Stefan Slater (*Prostitutes and Popular History: Note on the 'Underworld;' 1918 – 1939*) asserts that this link was never proved and, moreover, there was no evidence to show that the murders had been perpetrated by the Messina Brothers. What is certain is that organised prostitution was taken over by the Messina Brothers at the beginning of the war.

The five brothers were born in Valetta to a Sicilian father and a Maltese mother. The family name was Debono. Before coming to England, they had been linked to white slavery in Malta. As far back as 1908, Egyptian authorities were aware that they were forcing women into prostitution after luring them with promises of marriage. Once in Britain, the brothers quickly set about supplying women from Europe and by the end of the 1940s had thirty brothels in three seemingly respectable London streets. At this time,

Duncan Webb, a reporter from *The People* ran a series of exposés, which showed that the brothers had protection and information from Metropolitan Police officers. Interviews with prostitutes, as well as other crucial information was printed in the tabloid and this led to a formal investigation of the brothers' activities. The strangle hold the brothers had on crime was broken and they were forced to flee the country.

Many prostitutes did well out of the war however, but there were some whose misfortune it was to come across the mad or the bad, and when they did, it was usually not pretty.

The Blackout Ripper – Gordon Cummins, RAF, February 1942

Over time, there have been several serial murderers nicknamed, 'The Ripper'. Victorian Jack, of course, was never caught although his spree stopped after at least five victims in London. In recent times, Peter Sutcliffe, the so-called Yorkshire Ripper, was finally snared after killing thirteen women and attempting to kill seven more in a five-year period from 1975 to 1980. In the 1940s, there was another Ripper on the loose, a monster named Gordon Frederick Cummins, who exploited the blackout for his own bloody ends. Mercifully, his reign was short.

Cummings joined the RAF in 1935 as a Flight Rigger and married his wife Marjorie, the secretary to a theatre producer, the following year. At the outbreak of war, he was sent to No. 600 Squadron stationed at Helensburgh, Dunbartonshire. Here, having left Marjorie behind in Barnes at a flat she shared with her sister, he was a pub regular and very popular with the ladies, who were bowled over by his refined manner of speech and seemingly endless wads of cash. Simon Read mentions the 'intoxicating effect' he had on women (*Dark City*, 2010). In April 1941, he was posted to Colerne, Wiltshire, where he took to calling himself the 'Honourable Gordon Cummings'. He also began visiting a brothel in Bath, the Hole in the Wall, despite it being out of bounds to RAF personnel. It was while he was in Colerne that a woman was attacked in a neighbouring area, Ford. She managed to fight off her airman attacker, who tried to strangle her and rip her clothing off but she was not able to offer a description. Soon after, two more women were attacked, this time in Bath. Again, neither woman could give a description, other than that the attacker was an airman.

Just after he passed his pilot's test, the RAF posted Cummings to the Air Crew Receiving Centre in London's Regent's Park. He arrived there on 2 February 1942 and spent the night with a girl he picked up in Oxford Circus. It was the calm before the storm as he was about to go on a killing spree that would shock the nation and which the Head of Scotland Yard's Fingerprint Division, Chief Superintendent Frederick Cherrill, called an 'orgy of murder.'

On 9 February 1942, the body of a chemist's shop manager in Hornchurch was found in an air raid shelter in Montague Place, Marylebone, by a passing electrician, Harold Batchelor, on his way to work at eight o'clock in the morning.

From Newcastle Upon Tyne, Evelyn Hamilton had celebrated her forty-first birthday the day before. She had arrived in London late in the evening on 8 February and was last seen when taxi driver Abraham Ash dropped her at a hostel in Gloucester Place. Patrolling War Reserve Constable Arthur Williams checked the air raid shelter and found nothing untoward at 11.20pm that dark, moonless night. On his patrol, Williams did not notice anything happening at the shelter, even though he passed it several times. Bernard Spilsbury, the celebrated Home Office pathologist who had identified Dr Crippen as his wife's murderer years before, performed the post mortem examination. Evelyn had been manually strangled by a left handed killer. Later, on investigation, it was found that she had booked into a boarding house at 76 Gloucester Place, a short distance from where she was found, and gone out into the inky blackness to the local Lyons Corner House for a late meal. She had not returned. Police also noted that she had been robbed of the £80 in her purse. A man's linen handkerchief, embellished with the numbers 4 and 29 embroidered in red cotton, one on top of the other, was a clue to the murderer and by 5 March newspapers were appealing for information about it to help the police.

Before then though, there were more victims. On 10 February, the naked body of Evelyn Oatley was found. Thirty-five-year-old Oatley, also known as Leta Ward, was a budding actress married to a poultry farmer. She had left home for the bright lights of the London stage only to find those lights dimmed by the war. Out of financial necessity she had turned to prostitution and brought a steady stream of men to her tiny one-roomed flat in Wardour Street, partitioned from her neighbour, Ivy Poole, by two folding doors. Ivy had wondered at the sudden loudness of the music playing in Oatley's room but she did not like to make a fuss or disturb Evelyn and her client, so did not knock. A gruesome sight awaited Ivy when she did tap at Oakley's door with the men to empty the gas meter. Her throat had been cut with a razor blade, she had been strangled and, later, her body had been mutilated with a can opener and sexually violated. Spilsbury once more performed the autopsy and again noted that the killer was left handed. Frederick Cherrill, the expert in finger print technology, found finger prints on the can opener that confirmed this view.

With two murders to solve, Chief Inspector Edward (Ted) Greeno, from the colloquially-named 'Murder Squad' at Scotland Yard, was called in.

A highly respected police officer who was to receive eighty-six commissioners' commendations over his long career, Greeno joined the

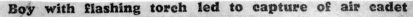

Boy with flashing torch led to capture of air cadet

MURDERER WITH THREE-WAY MIND POSED AS TITLED

Express Staff Reporter MONTAGUE LACEY

IN the mental make-up of Gordon Frederick Cummins, 28-year-old married air cadet, sentenced to death at the Old Bailey yesterday for murdering a woman, there were three personalities.

No. 1 was his normal life in the R.A.F. "A very intellectual type of airman," said his commanding officer when recommending him for promotion.

No. 2 was the vain young man known to his friends as "the duke" or "the count," who posed as the Hon. Gordon Cummins, acquired affected speech and boasted of his conquests with women.

No. 3 was the murderer, a man who, in the words of Mr. Justice Asquith was accused of

.... ..y on the evidence was built up, and at Bow-street Cummins was charged with the murder of :—

Mrs. Oatley ;
Mrs. Margaret Florence Lowe, aged 43—in Gosfield-street, W.;
Mrs. Doris Jouannet, aged 32, wife of an hotel manager—in Sussex-gardens, Paddington, W., and of
Miss Evelyn Hamilton, aged 40, a chemist, at Montagu-place, Marylebone, W.

The police said that in one night he murdered one woman and tried to murder two others. All the alleged murders were committed within a week.

RESEARCH CHEMIST

GORDON FREDERICK CUMMINS
"The Duke," "The Count," they called him.

Above: Gordon Frederick Cummins, the Blackout Ripper.

police force at the age of twenty in 1921. In 1923, he became Detective Greeno when he joined the Criminal Investigation Department (CID). He worked his way up through the ranks by way of the racecourses, where he waged war on those he called 'pests', the pickpockets and gang members infesting the meetings at the time. Later, he took on forgers and burglars, swindlers and fraudsters, but never murderers. In October 1940, he was promoted to Detective Chief Inspector and started to investigate murder cases. Greeno, described as a 'Master Detective' by Dick Kirby in his well-researched book, *The Guv'nors*, believed that solving a murder was akin to completing a jigsaw. One merely had to connect all the pieces. The trick was to find the pieces, the hidden clues, that built up a picture of the crime and who had perpetrated it. The Ripper case gave him plenty of pieces to collect.

The next bodies were found in quick succession. Margaret Florence Lowe died screaming, strangled by a left handed murderer and then mutilated, her body ripped open and violated. She was found, stiff and with back arched, in her flat in Gosfield Street, off the Tottenham Court Road. Bernard Spilsbury, once again called in, recognised the same handiwork to the first two murders and was to identify that same hand in the fourth, that of Doris Jouannet, the thirty-two-year-old wife of a seventy-year-old hotelier, who had been mutilated with a razorblade. The police understood that they had a serial killer on the streets. Greeno realised that the murders had been committed on consecutive days, Sunday, Monday, Tuesday and Thursday. Why, he wondered, was there a gap on Wednesday? He ramped up the police presence in the square mile in which the killer seemed to be operating. Three of the women were prostitutes, albeit, Jouannet was a part-timer, and so it was to the working girls on the street that Greeno first made enquiries. Greeno and Spilsbury had reached Jouannet while she was still warm, which meant that the murderer had not been far ahead of them. They soon found that while they were with her body, another girl, respectable but gullible Mary Heyward, was being attacked, in the West End, by the Captain's Cabin, near the Trocodero and Piccadilly. This time, the girl survived the kiss that masked the tightening of the hand around her throat. She was able to scream and there was a witness nearby, John Shine, who came to help. The victim was able to tell police that her attacker had wide-set green eyes, was an airman of about five feet seven inches in height and that she recognised his forage cap as being one for an officer cadet. In his haste to leave, the attacker dropped his gas mask. It had a service number stamped inside it, 525987, which was later identified as belonging to Gordon Cummings. Cummings was charged with assault to commit grievous bodily harm. Greeno though was suspicious and decided to look more closely at Cummings. In the meantime, enquiries amongst the street girls led to news of another Thursday night attack, this one timed between the murder of Jouannet and the attack in the West End. Phyllis O'Dwyer had told her friends about a mad punter, a RAF pilot cadet, who tried to strangle her with her own necklace. In her desperation to get away, she lashed out with her feet, clad in her only clothing, boots. They were to save her life as she knocked her attacker off the bed. She later reported that his wide-set green eyes had been blazing but he quietened down and said he was sorry. He had paid O'Dwyer £5 and paid her another £5 to apologise. It was two of the £1 notes he gave her that gifted Greeno another piece in the Blackout Ripper jigsaw puzzle. He was able to trace them because they were in sequence. In fact, Greeno was able to pin point the exact spot in the RAF pay parade that the notes were given out and established that they had been given to Cummings.

Greeno spoke to Cummings in Brixton jail. During the interview, Cummings explained away the gas mask by saying that he had been in the West End that night but his gas mask had got mixed up with that of another serviceman, so it must have been he who was the girl's attacker. He signed a statement to that affect, with his left hand.

Above: Air raid shelters appeared in city streets up and down the country and were often scenes of crime, such as pickpocketing... or worse.

Cummings' gas mask case had grit in it that could have come from the air raid shelter where the first victim had been killed on the Sunday evening. Cummings also had a wrist watch that was similar to one owned by Doris Jouannet, and it was padded at the back with Elastoplast. The strip fitted exactly to a gap in the roll in Jouannet's home. He was also in possession of a comb that fitted the dust pattern outline in Jouannet's flat, while in his uniform pocket a fountain-pen was found that fitted another dust space on the dead woman's mantelpiece. Her husband later positively identified all the items as belonging to his wife. A search of Cummings' billet produced a green propelling pencil borrowed by Evelyn Hamilton from a friend and a pair of rubber soles, which Cummings had removed from his boots because he thought that their distinctive treads would be traced back to him. It has been snowing on the night of the first murder …

It seemed that Greeno had his man. However, Cummings had a solid alibi for each night, in the form of the pass-book at his billet, which clearly indicated that he was there during the time of each attack. His roommates also swore that they saw him go to bed and get up again the following morning. What to do? Greeno soon found that the pass-book had been fabricated, with friends covering for absences by signing Cummings in when he was not actually on the premises. Another friend admitted that he had accompanied Cummings on a nocturnal trip after lights out, having gone to bed first to allay suspicion. The pair had then tiptoed down the fire escape. Cummings' alibi was shot to pieces.

Greeno later found another girl picked up by Cummings that Thursday night. She had been saved by her pimp, hiding behind a blanket screening the bed from the rest of the room. Cummings had spotted his watching eyes as he undressed, and left in a hurry. The man had undoubtedly saved the girl's life by being present.

Cummings had a large quantity of cash on him, which he had splashed liberally during the week, after claiming hardship and borrowing a pound from his wife the last time he saw her, on 8 February. Evelyn Hamilton was carrying £80 when she was killed and this was not recovered. He had showed Mary Heyward £30 in a wad, in a bid to entice her on to her back, and had bank rolled fellow RAF pilot cadets while out drinking. Circumstantial evidence against Cummings began to stack up. Greeno found that on Wednesday 12 February, the one night when there was not a murder, Cummings had been on duty and unable to leave his camp.

Gordon Frederick Cummings was charged with four counts of murder and two counts of attempted murder. He pleaded not guilty to each charge. He was tried for the murder of Evelyn Oatley at the Old Bailey. On 28 April 1942, the jury took just thirty-five minutes to find him guilty of murder. He was executed at Wandsworth Prison on 25 June. He was twenty-eight years of age.

There are no memorials to Gordon Cummins because the RAF, unlike the Army, had a policy of discharging men before they were executed.

Folkstone Blackout

Home Office Pathologist Professor Sir (Cedric) Keith Simpson, in his autobiography, *Forty years of Murder* (1978), recounts a sad tale of murder in the black out, which ended in an unexpected result.

On 17 June 1943, the body of Caroline Traylor (sometimes listed as Ellen, her middle name, in newspapers reporting the crime) was found in a bombed out shop, in Foord Road, Folkstone, four days after she had been reported missing by her mother. Caroline was an eighteen-year-old cinema usherette, had been married for just six months to Sgt Edgar Trayler of the Durham Light Infantry, and was bored with sitting in each evening with her mother, waiting for her husband to come home from the war. Craving diversion, and perhaps something more basic, she went out to the local pub, the Mechanic's Arms, in St Johns Street, where she was last seen leaving with a soldier at closing time.

Simpson was called in as soon as her body was found. The post mortem revealed that she had been strangled. It also showed that she had had sexual intercourse immediately before death. Simpson felt that, from the bruising evident on the body, the sex had started as consensual but that it had then turned to rape, and then to murder. Death had come quickly, perhaps in as little as twenty or thirty seconds.

Simpson found six dark hairs on Caroline's body, at stark contrast to her own auburn locks. From under her finger nails he found a rust-brown wool fibre.

The trail for the killer led to Manchester-born Dennis Leckey, a twenty-four-year-old family man and a gunner in the Royal Artillery, who had disappeared, Absent Without Leave, the day after Caroline's body was found. He was apprehended ten days later in London but refused to talk to the police. It was down to Simpson's expertise to build the case against him from the evidence provided from Caroline's body. A check of his clothes found that the wool fibre was the same as that of Leckey's uniform shirt, although it was noted that it was standard issue and so worn by thousands of service men at the time. The police forwarded body hairs from the suspect and these were confirmed as identical to the six hairs found adhering to Caroline's body. At the Metropolitan Police Laboratory, its Director, Dr Davidson, had found an auburn hair similar to Caroline's on the leg of Leckey's uniform trousers.

The jury at the Old Bailey took just half an hour of deliberations to pronounce Leckey guilty and he was duly sentenced to death by a black capped judge, Mr Justice Singleton.

However, in a strange twist of fate, Leckey was successfully able to appeal the verdict and sentence because the Court of Criminal Appeal agreed that Singleton had led the jury when he noted the defendant's lack of co-operation with the police in his summing up. Three times he had implied that the silence suggested guilt. As this was tantamount to misdirecting the jury, the conviction was quashed and Leckey was freed. One newspaper noted that Leckey had 'remained unmoved throughout the proceedings' (*Western Daily Press*, 2 November 1943).

The blackout undoubtedly aided the criminal on the war-torn Home Front. On a practical level, the darkness proved a boon to the burglar, intent on entering a property without being seen, and offered opportunity and gave cover to those up to no good when out on the street. A generation of children grew up thinking that the blackout each night was the norm, while their mothers fought to get the curtains up in time. For those who failed, the law came down swiftly.

Above: The murder rate went up by twenty-two percent during the Second World War as pent-up grievances or the stress of war took their toll. Murderers often took advantage of wartime conditions, including bombing raids and their aftermath, to cover up their grisly misdeeds. It was easy to hide, or discard, a body in the rubble of a bombed building.

4

> The huge stresses and strains of
> simply getting through each day
> brought simmering tensions to
> the fore, ready to overflow and
> spill out into violence.

Murder

The Concise Oxford Dictionary offers the following definitions for
'*murder*':
Noun: The unlawful premediated killing of a human being by another
Verb: 1 Kill (a human being) unlawfully, esp, wickedly or inhumanly
2 *Law* kill; (a human being) with a premeditated motive.

The murder rate went up by twenty-two percent during the period 1941 -
45. It might seem strange to a twenty-first century audience that this should
be the case. After all, most of the country was busy fighting for freedom,
wasn't it? Why chose now, when there were so many crises to deal with, to
kill someone? Inspecting some murder cases from the era gives more
insight. The huge stresses and strains of simply getting through each day
brought simmering tensions to the fore, ready to overflow and spill out into
violence. For some murderers, using bombing raids to cover up murder
seemed a perfect idea. For others, the authority that came with certain
wartime positions gave opportunities that peacetime simply did not offer.
Extra pressure also came along with the break-up of family units, men
drafted away to fight; children evacuated and women spending long hours
in often dangerous jobs. Loneliness also played its part, with the need for
companionship, or plain old-fashioned sex, bringing out the bad, the
unscrupulous or the unprincipled. In short, the fact that the country was
plunged into a turmoil that dragged on for six long years led to many more
people committing the ultimate crime.

Molly Lefebure (1919 – 2013), known to Metropolitan police officers as
'Molly of the Morgue', in her matter of fact recounting of her life as the
secretary to Britain's famous wartime pathologist, Sir Keith Simpson,
Murder on the Home Front (1954), makes a point about murderers in
wartime. She gives the example of the January 1944 case of the death of a
housekeeper, Klara Steindl, a forty-seven-year-old refugee, who was unlucky

.... the case was destined to remain unsolved. The reason? The suspects had been conscripted and sent overseas to fight. They were therefore out of British police jurisdiction and so, literally, were able to use the war to get away with murder.

enough to be employed by a wealthy Greek ship owner who had several safes in his house in Surrey. Burglars heard about the promise of riches in the house and waited until the owner was abroad before breaking in to steal the contents of those enticing vaults. To do this, they had to neutralise the housekeeper. Klara was hit over the head, trussed up and gagged and left in the hallway while the burglars went about their business. They then left her, bound and gagged, and escaped. Klara, struggling to free herself, found it harder and harder to breathe. The gag, the injuries to her head and her desperation to escape all combined to asphyxiate her. She was found some while later, blue in the face. Police enquiries soon led to suspects and for some little while the investigation went well. However, the case was destined to remain unsolved. The reason? The suspects had been conscripted and sent overseas to fight. They were therefore out of British police jurisdiction and so, literally, were able to use the war to get away with murder. This case was one of the first where the murderer escaped the hand of the law by being conscripted.

Escalating crime

The blackout and earning cash from the Black Market were to lead one gang of young crooks into trouble they did not see coming. Frank Greenaway, an 18-year-old unemployed tester and weighman with a wasted right leg due to the effects of infantile paralysis at the age of thirteen; Colin Geoffrey Gray, an 18-year-old labourer; Felix John Jenkins, a nineteen-year-old clerk in a garage from a Lithuanian family and Edward Alfred Hare, a labourer aged 18 were out for what they could get in a spree that ended with jail terms for all four. At the time the offences were committed, the group had known each other for less than three weeks.

Robert Lewis Dockerill, a Tottenham shop assistant was hard up and so sold his 1917 Luger .38 automatic to Felix Jenkins for £3. Frank Greenaway suggested that the gang cruise the blacked out streets in a car Jenkins had taken from his employer's premises, offering people they met a lift in the car and then robbing them at gun point. This seemed like a good idea and so, on 13 October 1940, they picked up Ernst Israel Altmann, 'a foreigner' (National Archives: CRIM 1/1267). Mr Altmann was the German manager of a firm of waste paper merchants. At 10.30 that evening, he had been waiting for a bus in Seven Sisters Road when the gang's car pulled up and he was asked if he would like a lift. He asked for a ride to Edmonton. While Greenaway held him up at gun point, Gray relieved him of his wallet containing £5.10.0 and a wrist watch.

On 17 October 1940, at 9pm, the gang decided to rob the off-licence section of the Alexandra Park Tavern in Wood Green. It was pouring with rain and an air raid was just beginning. Jenkins went in first, to see the lay of the land. Inside, behind the counter, were forty-three-year-old Gwendolyn Louisa Wehrmann, known as Miss Cox, following her divorce from an Australian soldier, and Anne Marian Higgin, the bar maid. Business was slow and the pair were chatting. Visible overhead were pound notes in a glass jar. Jenkins asked for a packet of Player's Weights cigarettes and was told that they only had Woodbines. Jenkins left but came back almost immediately, with a black cloth around his mouth and two of the gang to back him up. Greenway had been left in the car's driving seat as he was less agile than the rest. Jenkins produced the Luger and told the women to put their hands up. Miss Cox thought it was a joke and lent forward to slap his wrist with a bottle. The gun went off, killing her instantly. The three fled, Hare still clinging to the running board of the getaway car as it roared away. A witness, coffee stallholder Edward Zugg, was able to identify the car as a 1937 Studebaker saloon.

The gang broke into and entered the firm of S Gray Ltd., in Silver Street, Edmonton that same evening. They stole 22 wireless sets to the value of £73.1.0. These they took to the nearby Hills Café, where 15 of the sets were sold on to five unidentified men who arrived by car, for the sum of £18. Each member of the gang received £4.10.0. Jenkins kept the last wireless for himself.

The police investigation was led by Ted Greeno, on his first murder enquiry, who ordered an all-night manhunt for the gang from Stamford Hill to Edmonton. It paid off. Greenaway had not been able to resist showing the gun to a friend a few days before the killing. The friend he had boasted to spoke to the police and it was then only a matter of time before the whole motley crew were rounded up.

All pleaded guilty to manslaughter at the Old Bailey. Jenkins and Greenaway were each sentenced to three years' penal servitude. Gray and Hare went to jail for eighteen months.

A Naval Hero

To risk a robbery in broad daylight at a busy time when any number of witnesses were about was to commit a crime regardless of consequences. Organised crime struck in London and a man paid for their callous greed with his life.

Above: Capt. Ralph Binney CBE

It is certain that Royal Navy Captain Ralph Douglas Binney did not start his last day on earth with the idea of ending it as a hero. These things often happen on the spur of the moment. On this day, Friday 8 November 1944, the fifty-six-year-old First World War veteran, who had been awarded the CBE the year previously, who lost his son, David, in the war and who was described as 'a lovely, lovely guy' by his great-niece, Caroline Brodrick, simply found himself at the wrong place at the wrong time and instinct took over. He was to pay for this with his life.

Birchin Lane is a narrow thoroughfare not far from the Bank of England in the City of London. In 1944, Frank Wordley had his jeweller's shop at number 23 and business was as normal as it could be given the wartime conditions. Shoppers bustling by that foggy day were shocked to find themselves witnessing a smash and grab raid on the shop that turned into an horrific murder. A Vauxhall 14 car stopped outside the building. A passing bank clerk later put the time of day at 2pm. Two men got out and one of them used the axe he was carrying to smash the shop's display windows. They calmly helped themselves to the expensive trinkets for sale: a pearl necklace and fourteen rings, three of which were later found in the back of the abandoned car. They then hotfooted it back to the car before

Above: Birchin Lane, the scene of the robbery that claimed the life of Capt. Binney.

they could be apprehended. Making their getaway down the lane towards Lombard Street, they did not stop for Captain Binney, who, his sense of duty coming to the fore, stepped out into the car's path to block their escape route. The brave captain, who had been called out of retirement at the outbreak of the war and was recently returned from a stint in Alexandria as Flag Captain at HMS Nile, was now stationed in London. He no doubt thought that the driver would hesitate to drive at a person in the road and so gestured for the driver to stop. He did not realise that he was dealing with a member of the notorious Elephant Boys gang from the Elephant and Castle area of the city. He was callously knocked down and run over in the robbers' flight. Onlookers ran to stop the car and to help the stricken man. In doing so, they blocked the robbers' route. Panicking, the driver reversed the car and ran over Captain Binney once more, only to find that there was no escape back down the lane as more horrified witnesses were coming forward to stop them. Throwing the car forward once more, they ran over Captain Binney for a third time and, forcing a path, they sped away, being chased by a passing motorist who witnessed the events. This time though, their victim's clothing was caught under the car and he was dragged for over a mile, still conscious and frantically screaming for help, along Lombard Street, over London Bridge to London Bridge Station, where he finally freed himself and rolled into the gutter. He was mortally injured, his crushed lungs having been stabbed by his broken ribs. He died just three hours later at Guy's Hospital.

A huge manhunt followed. There were five involved in the raid on the jeweller. One person was acting as lookout and four were in the car (National Archives file CRIM 1/1655). The police were determined to get their men and staked out working men's clubs and pubs in the area in an effort to find those responsible for the murder. Eventually, information led them to Thomas James Jenkins, a welder, arrested at a social club in Woking on 22 December, who swore he was not the driver. This was twenty-six year-old Ronald Hedley, a labourer and serial burglar. He was picked up at 51 Jamaica Road, Bermondsey on 27 December. The car had been found abandoned in Tooley Street. On investigation, it was found that, with four average men sitting inside, there was a clearance of just seven inches at the front axle and six and a half inches at the rear.

Their trial concluded on 12 March 1945 after six days of evidence. Hedley was found guilty of murder and sentenced to hang. Jenkins was found guilty of manslaughter and given eight years' penal servitude. Hedley appealed but this was dismissed on 13 April. However, on 26 April, just two days before he was due to be executed, he was reprieved by the Home Secretary and sentenced to life imprisonment. He served nine years and was released, aged thirty-five, in 1954.

Above: From left to right: David Crompton, Chief Constable South Yorkshire Police, host of the Police Public Bravery Awards (PPBA); Sara Thornton, Head of the National Police Chief's Council (NPCC); Caroline Brodrick, Binney's great-niece and the presenter of the Binney Award; Taylor Hughes, the recipient of the 2016 award; Rear Admiral Dick Melly, Clerk of the Goldsmiths Hall.

Caroline says, *"The Binney Awards were hosted in fine pomp in Goldsmith's Great Hall, with the Lord Mayor and sometimes royalty presenting the medals. Since 2008, the PPBA host a reception there every year for present and all past Binney award winners. Some turn up who won their medals in the 50s!"*

In 1947, fellow officers, friends of Ralph Binney, set in place a trust fund to establish the Binney Award for bravery. It is awarded for the bravest action in support of law and order performed in the areas controlled by the Metropolitan or City of London Police by a person not a member of a police force. Now part of the Police Public Bravery Awards, instituted in 1965, Caroline Brodrick, Binney's great-niece, presents it annually at a ceremony at Goldsmiths' Hall, City of London, to the person the Police Public Bravery Committee considers to be the most outstanding of the winners. In 2016 the award was presented to Taylor Hughes. His citation reads:

National Police Public Bravery Awards 2016

Restricted

NOMINATION 5

Nominee: Taylor Hughes/ Jack Purcell

Age: 16/17 years

Force: Cheshire Police

Circumstances

At approximately 5.35pm on Saturday 8th November 2014, a 41-year-old female was repeatedly stabbed by a 49-year-old man on Lower Appleton Road, Widnes. During the attack, the female sustained life threatening injuries. On witnessing this attack, 16-year-old Taylor Hughes got out of the vehicle he was travelling in and approached the offender who was leaning over the victim on the ground. At this time, the offender was repeatedly stabbing the victim with a kitchen knife. Taylor selflessly intervened by kicking the offender in the shoulder area to stop him stabbing the victim. This had the desired effect and caused the offender to stop the attack. The offender then began to move towards Taylor, still holding the knife in his hand. At this point, the victim was able to get to her feet and make her way into a newsagents where an ambulance was called. The offender then turned and calmly walked away from the scene, holding the knife. Taylor began to follow him from a safe distance and shouted after him. He then saw one of his friends, Jack Purcell, walking on the opposite side of the road, and shouted to him, instructing him to call the police. Taylor told Jack that the man he was following had just stabbed a female. As a direct result of this information, Jack immediately contacted the police using his mobile phone and, without consideration for their own safety, both boys continued to follow the offender. Taylor was shouting at the offender whilst Jack spoke to the police operator, giving clear and concise information regarding the offender and their exact location. On a number of occasions whilst following him, the offender turned and ran back in the direction of Taylor, lunging towards him with the knife. Taylor and Jack backed away quickly, preventing the offender from reaching them. Jack maintained his commentary with the police operator whilst Taylor continued to shout towards the offender.

As a result of both Taylor's and Jack's actions, police officers were able to locate and detain the offender without any other people being injured.

Police officers attended the scene and provided first aid to the victim ahead of paramedics arriving. The female was then rushed to hospital, where she underwent emergency surgery to repair the damage caused by the multiple stab wounds sustained during the horrific attack,

Had it not been for Taylor's quick thinking and intervention in the initial attack and Jack's detailed commentary whilst they followed the offender, the victim may not have survived and the offender may have not been detained so promptly. Their joint actions led to the quick detention and arrest of the offender, thus preventing any further attack on anyone else and ensuring vital evidence was secured.

Capt. Binney seems to have left behind a legacy that is enduring.

The decision to commute Hedley's death sentence was later claimed to be a major factor in the rise of armed gangs after the war.

Child Murder

Murder always leaves a rotten taste in the mouth but the murder of children is particularly heinous. Sadly, the six years of the Second World War was not a time when children were safe from murder, any more than their parents were.

Ted Greeno reported the murder of eleven-year-old Sheila Margaret Wilson in his biography *War on the Underworld*. In Lewisham, on Monday 20 July 1942, Sheila had gone to run an errand for a man down the road, who had asked her to go and get an evening newspaper for him. It was 8.35 at night and her bedtime was at 9, but she just had time to nip out and perform the good deed. As she left her home, her mother urged her to hurry, it was getting late. It was the last conversation they had. Her distraught mother reported her missing at 11pm, having scoured the area they lived in, looking for her to no avail.

One of the first people the police spoke to in their routine enquiries was thirty-eight-year-old ARP stretcher-bearer Edward Kingston. He lodged just a few doors from the Wilson family with Mr and Mrs Graham and their family. He had been caught in a 1940 air raid and walked with a limp as a result. Kingston ended up on a shortlist of two suspects for the disappearance, the other being a member of the Fire Service. Both men lived in the same street as Sheila, but Kingston claimed never to have spoken to her. This struck Greeno as odd. Surely, in such a small community, he would have spoken to her. He had lived there for eight of

Sheila's eleven years. Greeno was about to bring him in for questioning when it was learnt that Kingston was missing. He had said that he was going to the hospital on Saturday to have his leg examined; he claimed to have banged it on a chair and made it bleed. Two days later, he still had not returned. Kingston had been off duty the day that Sheila had gone missing …

Greeno had the house searched from top to bottom. In the space under the house, accessed by a trapdoor in the hall, the police found a pile of rubble under the base of the chimney stack. Buried underneath, they found little Sheila. She had been strangled with a window cord, which was wound around her neck three times. She had also been sexually assaulted.

Greeno was determined to get his man and had police officers stay in the house round the clock in the hope that Kingston would return. In a time when police manpower was a scarce commodity, it was a huge undertaking. Nevertheless, it was worthwhile. On Wednesday, the tell-tale thump, thump sound of the limping murderer returning home was heard. He was immediately arrested. When asked why he had come back, he said that he owed Mr Graham a pound, which he wanted to repay.

Kingston later explained the murder by saying, "I know it was wrong … and I must pay for it. When she … said what paper did I want I said I didn't want a paper at all, I just wanted to kiss and cuddle her. She started to scream and … I went mad," (Greeno). He had damaged his bad leg when he dragged her body into the hall, lifted the lino and the trapdoor and buried her in the rubble. Police found traces of the rubble in his trouser turn-ups.

On 14 September 1942, at the Old Bailey, Kingston was sentenced to death for the murder of Sheila Wilson.

The Babes in the Wood – Doreen Hearne and Kathleen Trendall

These two little girls were also victims of someone they should have been able to trust. The Metropolitan Police case file was closed for seventy-five years after the case and will not be opened until 1 January 2018. However, the criminal case file (CRIM 1/1376) is available to read at the National Archives. It is not for the faint hearted as it contains upsetting images and details.

Doreen Hearne was eight and little Kathleen Trendle was just six when they met their end in Rough Park, Amersham, Buckinghamshire on 19 November 1941. They had both left home after dinner at 12.50 to go back to school. Doreen had a hair ribbon in her hair and carried a gas mask. Kathleen carried a red gas mask case. They had asked a soldier in an army lorry for a lift after Tylers Green Council School finished for the day, and had happily been driven off by him. Several of their friends had seen them ask for the lift and watched them ride away. They did not arrive home. At 5pm, the vehicle was seen in a lane near Rough Wood, Amersham.

On 20 November 1941, a pink ribbon was found on the ground in Rough Wood. At 3pm, the regiment's drivers belonging to 341 Battery Royal Artillery, stationed in Hazlemere Park, Amersham, were put on parade. Five children walked down the parade of men and one child, twelve-year-old Norman Page, picked out one man, wearing a pair of horn-rimmed spectacles, as the driver of the vehicle whom the two girls had asked for a lift. Harold Hill, the driver picked out, was a twenty-six-year-old soldier with five previous convictions, including for assault on a female in 1931 and on a female under sixteen in 1932. He had been called up on 1 September 1939. He usually wore steel-rimmed glasses issued by the Army.

The mileage log for the vehicle Hill had been driving on 19 November showed a discrepancy between it and the mileage on the dashboard. There were an extra 43 miles on the clock. Hill could only account for 20 of them. He was the regular driver for the 15cwt 'Fordson' truck, which could only be moved after a work ticket had been issued for the journey to the driver, signed by an officer. Hill's lorry had a leak in the back axle and oil would leak where it was parked for any length of time. Hill's clothing was damp and a tarpaulin in the truck had a piece cut out of it.

On the day of the children's murder, Hill had been part of a fatigue party tidying up the camp. He went to the toilet between 4 and 4.15 and said he was completing maintenance on the lorry after that. There were no witnesses to this, or to the fact that he said he went to tea at 5pm. After tea he went to fill up but, he did not fill up his own vehicle, this was full already he claimed. He was seen at the fuel pump between 7pm and 7.15 but he was filling a vehicle whose usual driver was on leave. Hill was in the guardroom later when the police arrived with a little girl, Irene May Jaques, who picked Hill out as the person she saw driving the lorry the girls went away in. Hill was, at that time, wearing his own horn-rimmed spectacles, not the steel-rimmed pair the army had issued him.

The next day, Stephen Edwin Baker, another driver, took over Hill's vehicle and found it needed fuel. He filled it with eight gallons of diesel.

On 22 November, the two girls' blood-soaked bodies were found in the wood by Christopher Mason, a Patrol Leader with the Tenth High Wycombe Scouts. A sock was found five feet from the ground in the branch of a tree

> **Five children walked down the parade of men and one child, twelve-year-old Norman Page, picked out one man, wearing a pair of horn-rimmed spectacles, as the driver of the vehicle whom the two girls had asked for a lift.**

and a red gas mask case was nearby. The girls had been strangled to unconsciousness and then bludgeoned to death. The sadistic crimes seemed motiveless.

On 23 November, a respirator in a case was found in a clump of ferns just three yards from the foot path leading to Mop Lane, where an army lorry had been parked with its hood up at 5.05pm on 19 November. The case had Doreen's name and address on it.

Metropolitan Police Superintendent Frederick Cherril was in charge of the fingerprint bureau at New Scotland Yard. He was able to identify a finger print on the red gas mask case found by the bodies as belonging to Hill. A handkerchief also found at the scene was identified by its laundry mark.

Several children came forward as witnesses to the girls getting into the lorry with the soldier. One of them, Brenda Teadsdale, aged 12, was able to give police a partial number plate: 43JP, which corresponded to Hill's lorry.

Hill admitted knowing the children in the guardroom when asked but said that he had not picked them up and had not been out that day. The police officer questioning him had not said when the girls had disappeared. Hill's denim blouse and battle dress trousers were found to be blood stained on examination. The knife used in the attack on the girls was later found in the woods where the bodies were discovered.

Hill was charged with the murder of Doreen Hearne and his trial at the Central Criminal Court, Old Bailey began on 3 February 1942. He was found guilty and sentenced to death. His appeal, on 17 April 1942, was unsuccessful and he was executed at Oxford on 1 May 1942.

The funerals of Doreen Hearne and Kathleen Trendall took place on Thursday 27 November 1941. Thousands turned out to pay their respects.

Afternoon Tea ... and Murder

Going out for afternoon tea is a quintessentially British thing to do. The Lyons Corner House, long a staple on High Streets up and down the country, was the obvious place to go for those who wanted quality at a decent price.

The first Lyons Corner House, every restaurant had two entrances, each on a different road, was opened in 1894 and was a product of the collaboration of four far-sighted entrepreneurs, Joseph Lyons, Isidore and Montague Gluckstein and Barnett Salmon. Their vision was to lead to a catering empire that became the largest in Europe, encompassing hotels, tea plantations, ice cream, tea and coffee companies and engineering works amongst many others. In the process, their company 'J Lyons and Co.' was to become a household name and their waitresses, known as 'Nippies,' nationally loved. The Joe Lyons tearoom was, literally, a corner of respectability.

The company did its bit during the war, too. As the excellent history of the company on www.kzwp.com/lyons points out, as well as managing a bomb-making factory and producing war materials, J Lyons and Co. also produced the rations for many of the British front line troops, particularly those in Asia. American servicemen stationed in Grosvenor Square benefitted, too, from the Lyons' bequest of a London tearoom.

On 20 April 1945, 250 or so people had decided to go the Lyons Corner House on Oxford Street, London. No one took notice of the family group enjoying their tea and chat. Why should they? They were just the same as everyone else there that day, relaxing, hopeful that the end of the war was in sight.

He arrived to find John Baptiste Tratsart lying dead from two gunshots, Claire dying and Hugh seriously injured. The entire tearoom clientele were shocked, but none had seen a thing.

The Tratsart family had assembled to discuss returning to their family home in Norbury, south London, from their evacuation quarters in Northampton. The eldest son, 27-year-old Jacques (Jack) Adrian Tratsart had remained behind in Norbury and it was his idea for the family to get together that fateful day. Around the table with Jack were his father John Baptiste, aged 57, a Belgian shoe designer, who had come to Britain before the First World War; sister Claire, aged 28 and an epileptic; younger brother Hugh who was semi-paralysed; 13-year-old sister Ann and his aunt, Miss Claire Mary Coemans, Jack's late mother's sister.

'Higgins of the Yard,' Detective Inspector Robert Higgins, was the detective called to deal with the aftermath of the cosy family chat over tea. In his behind-the-scenes biography, *In the Name of the Law* (1958) he tells the story. He arrived to find John Baptiste Tratsart lying dead from two gunshots, Claire dying and Hugh seriously injured. The entire tearoom clientele were shocked, but none had seen a thing. It was true that one or two had noticed the gun in Jack's hands but the family seemed relaxed about it, so they did not worry. It was only when the shots rang out that the screaming started and everyone dived for cover, thus missing the actual crime. Jack, after discovering how to cock the revolver, which he had purchased 'from a sailor' for £5 two years before, had lost no time in shooting his father, Claire and Hugh twice each, before trying to shoot himself - only the fact that there were no bullets left in the magazine prevented suicide.

Higgins records that 'the staff at the Corner House responded magnificently in the emergency and were most helpful to the police'. They screened off the family's table and would not allow anyone to leave until the police had released them. Needless to say, no further refreshments were served on that floor that day. Jack was under the guard of two soldiers when Higgins arrived and a uniformed police officer was the first on the scene. No one though had thought about making sure that Jack was disarmed and he himself was not going to make it easy to find the murder weapon, which was not evident from a search of the immediate area. Higgins eventually found the revolver in the glass wall light on a nearby pillar.

Why did the unmarried toolmaker decide to kill three members of his family and do so in such a public place? Higgins spent much time talking to him and his statement covered five typed pages. In an era when Hitler's views on those with disabilities led to the mass murder of the infirm, Jack Tratsart's ideas on the prospects for his sister and brother are chilling. Quite simply, he felt that because of their ailments their lives were already over. He had contemplated killing himself for several years and had finally decided that the best thing would be to do so and also put his sister and brother out of the misery he felt their lives were to them. While he was about it, he would kill his father, too, for being miserly and only interested in earning money.

At the table, he had twice pointed the gun at his sister and pulled the trigger but nothing had happened. When asked what he was doing he had joked that the gun was a water pistol. In reality, he had not set the cocking mechanism and so the gun would not fire. Everyone had laughed and continued chatting, completely oblivious to the danger they were in once he had figured out how the gun worked.

Higgins charged Jack Tratsart with two counts of murder and one of attempted murder. Although he was sent for trial at the Old Bailey, he was deemed to be insane and so did not stand trial. He died in Broadmoor high security psychiatric hospital two years later.

John George Haigh, the Acid Bath Murderer

"Mrs Durand-Deacon no longer exists. I have destroyed her with acid.' So confessed John George Haigh, after asking Detective Inspector Webb what the chances were of being released from Broadmoor, the hospital for the criminally insane (Dunboyne, *The Trial of John George Haigh*, 1953).

The confession came after damning evidence was found in a lock up in Horsham visited by Haigh, in the shape of a dry cleaning receipt for a Persian lamb coat, which was subsequently retrieved and identified as belonging to the missing woman, and an admission that he had sold her jewellery to a jeweller in Reigate. It was February 1949 and detectives were about to learn just how deadly the seemingly mild-looking John Haigh could be.

Above: John George Haigh, the Acid Bath Murderer.

In a statement given on 28 February that took two and a half hours to write, Haigh confessed to killing William Donald McSwan in 1944 at 79 Gloucester Road, SW7 and Donald and Amy McSwan, William's parents, the following year at the same address. He continued by confessing to the 1948 murders of Dr Archibald Henderson and his wife Rosalie at the store room he rented for 'experimental purposes' in Leopold Road, Crawley.

In each case, Haigh used the same method of disposing of the bodies – an acid bath.

He had met William McSwan, for whom he had worked as a chauffeur and secretary in 1936 when McSwan ran an amusement arcade, at the Goat Public House in Kensington High Street. The two men reminisced and McSwan mentioned that he had sold his amusement arcade when war broke out and invested the proceeds in other property. The pair often met up after this and also visited McSwan's parents, who were delighted to see him once again. 'Mac,' as McSwan was nicknamed, confided that he had a plan to avoid the draft by dropping out of sight and going underground. Haigh had fallen in love with Barbara, his boss's daughter at the light engineering firm he had been working for since leaving prison and asked 'Mac' to write a postcard to her for him in shorthand. The card, headed, 'Barbara Darling' gives no hint of the horrors to come as it deals with how fed up Haigh is because Barbara is away. 'Mac' wrote his own postscript, saying, 'John's let my cocoa get cold.' The whole reads as light-hearted banter between friends, a jolly wheeze to send a note to a girlfriend that her father will not be able to read. The card is postmarked 6 September 1944.

For some time, Haigh reportedly had dreams about blood, specifically, about drinking blood, and it was the desire to drink blood that allegedly led to the murder of his friend, McSwan. Haigh invited him back to his rented basement workshop at 79 Gloucester Road on 9 September 1944. Here he hit him with a cosh, cut his throat and 'withdrew a glass of blood from his throat and drank it,' (Dunboyne, *The Trial of John George Haigh*, 1953). He claimed to have done the same with Mrs Durand-Deacon. Within five minutes, the unfortunate McSwan was dead and was soon dissolved in a forty-gallon barrel of sulphuric acid. The resulting sludge was poured away down a drain. Lord Dunboyne, in his account of Haigh's story, opined that this was probably his first murder. Haigh looted the dead man of his identity card, wallet and sundry items before disposing of his body and told his parents that their son had gone away to avoid being called up for active service. Haigh went to great lengths to keep this charade going, writing a letter to McSwan's parents purporting to be from their son and posting it from Glasgow. He used the letter to give instructions on the disposal of properties owned by McSwan.

Haigh confessed later to the murder of a middle aged woman in similar circumstances to McSwan about two months after the first murder. However, there was no evidence of this crime and Haigh was vague as to detail, so the claim could not be verified.

Mr and Mrs McSwan were not seen at all after 2 July 1945. Each was invited to the basement workshop and met a fate identical to that of their son. Haigh explained that he had killed Mrs McSwan because he could not get enough blood to drink from the body of Mr McSwan. In his confession, Haigh said that there was a file in his hotel room which detailed all of the properties he had disposed of after their deaths. This showed a well-thought out and patiently executed plan to loot the family's assets, involving Haigh impersonating his dead friend McSwan and forging his signature on a Power of Attorney, which allowed him to sell four residential properties for £1,720 net, furniture, jewellery and effects for £4,000, as well as gilt-edged securities valued at £2,107. He also confessed to having obtained extra ration cards by using their identity cards to apply for new as if they were still alive. What seems fantastic to a twenty-first century audience is the fact that the family's disappearance went unnoticed and unreported. If Haigh had not confessed to the murders, he might have got away with them indefinitely.

Haigh further confessed to murdering a youth called Max in the autumn of 1945, but, again, there was not enough evidence for police to ascertain the truth of this.

Property seems to have been the main motive for the murders in each case. The Hendersons were shot in 1948, when Haigh's bank account was again overdrawn, 'From each of them I took my draught of blood,' Haigh is recorded as saying (Dunboyne). Their bodies were consumed by acid to obtain their home, which was then sold on, Haigh having forged the documents needed to obtain the deeds. Each victim was looted and their cigarette case, watch and jewellery, including Mrs Henderson's wedding and diamond engagement rings, were sold for £300 to a jeweller in Horsham. The total figure added to the Haigh bank account during 1948 was £7,771. To explain their disappearance to family, Haigh forged a letter to Mrs Henderson's brother, telling him that they had decided to emigrate to South Africa. He knew though that this would probably only hold back suspicion for a while and he was right. On 21 February 1949, the day that Haigh was busy selling Mrs Durand-Deacon's jewellery, Mrs Henderson's brother appealed for her to get in touch via the BBC as their mother was seriously ill. It would have been only a matter of time before he went to the police and they started their investigation of the disappearances.

On 4 March 1949, Haigh confessed to killing the woman from Hammersmith; Max, the youth from Kensington, once again at the address at 79 Gloucester Road, and Mary, a girl from Eastbourne. These confessions brought the tally of his alleged victims to nine, although he was charged with only one murder, that of Mrs Olive Henrietta Olivia Robarts Durand-Deacon.

This lady had been living quietly at the Onslow Court Hotel in South Kensington for six years. She was a well-to-do widow of independent means, who was friendly with another resident in similar circumstances, Mrs Constance Lane. The two saw each other daily and it was Mrs Lane who raised the alarm when her friend did not make an appearance at dinner on 18 February and was still not to be seen the following morning. A fellow guest at the hotel asked her if Mrs Durand-Deacon was sick as she had not shown up for an outing with him the previous day. It was this gentleman, John George Haigh, who drove Mrs Lane to the Chelsea police station and together they reported Mrs Durand-Deacon missing.

Enquiries soon revealed that Haigh, the neatly dressed, moustachioed gentleman with the matinee idol good looks, was not quite as he made out, having been convicted of several counts of dishonesty stretching over a period of years. He was convicted of conspiracy to defraud; aiding and abetting the forgery of a document and obtaining money by false pretences, with six other cases taken into consideration and was sentenced to fifteen months in jail in 1934. For obtaining money under false pretences he was sentenced to four years' penal servitude in 1937. He was released on licence in August 1940 and became a firewatcher, horrified by the sights he witnessed of war on the home front. It was while in jail once more, this time for stealing sixty yards of curtaining and a refrigerator, that he first started to experiment using acid to dissolve the bodies of mice supplied by prisoners who worked out in the fields. While working in the tinsmith's shop at Lincoln Prison, he came to understand the volume of acid needed to decompose a body and the length of time it took to reduce it to sludge. When he left prison, in September 1943, he was an expert on the subject.

By the time Mrs Durand-Deacon disappeared, Haigh had run through the monies obtained from the Hendersons. He tried to pay the £50 outstanding on his hotel bill with a cheque that bounced. It was later revealed that he was £83 5s 10d overdrawn at the bank and owed over £350 in gaming debts. Mrs Durand-Deacon was seen talking to him about the commercial possibilities of artificial fingernails on 14 February. Over the

Above: Interested members of the public watch as the Police search for clues to the Acid Bath Murder case at the premises of Hurstlea Products Ltd.

next few days, Haigh arranged for acid to be ordered and delivered to him at a storehouse in Crawley; tried to interest Mr Jones, the Managing Director of Hurstlea Products Limited, in producing the fingernails and succeeded in borrowing £50 from him, which he used to pay his hotel bill, and followed up 'a telephonic order' for sulphuric acid with a written confirmation to Mssers. White, a manufacturing chemist in London. On 17 February, Haigh then returned to Mr Jones with a stirrup pump and a request to have the foot sawn off. Without the foot, the pump was slim enough to fit down the neck of the carbouy, or demijohn, the acid was delivered in. That same day, receipts and eyewitnesses proved that Haigh took delivery of a black 40-gallon drum and he later exchanged it for a green one, able to resist acid corrosion. The stage was now set for a ninth murder.

Mrs Durand-Deacon was last seen at the Onslow Court Hotel at 2.15, with the handbag that was later found at the murder scene. The last sighting of her was at 4pm, when she and Haigh were observed at the George Hotel in Crawley. At 4.45 pm, Mr Jones received a call from Haigh to tell him that the person interested in producing the plastic finger nails had failed to turn up for their meeting. Haigh was still in Crawley later that day, being seen at the storeroom the acid was delivered to; eating egg on toast at Ye Olde Ancient Priors Restaurant and later entering the restaurant at the George Hotel. The next day, he played out the charade with Mrs Lane that eventually led to his downfall.

At Haigh's trial, a 'shopping list' of items was produced, which was identified as being written by Haigh, and which listed the items he needed to purchase to carry out the latest murder. Evidence from the scene identified the remnants in the barrel as being body parts belonging to the unfortunate lady: a gall stone, a jaw fragment and parts of a foot, and items belonging to her: a purse, lipstick holder, a notebook, hairpin, pen and holder and a powder compact. The fact that there was no body, a point that Haigh had relied on to save him from conviction, was suddenly irrelevant, particularly as the body parts had been identified as belonging to Mrs Durand-Deacon by Dr Keith Simpson, the Home Office Pathologist. Haigh's confession, minus the details about drinking the victim's blood, was read out to the jury. They were asked to decide if Haigh was guilty of murder or if he was guilty but insane. Just seventeen minutes' deliberations led to the jury giving a 'Guilty of Murder' decision. John Haigh kept his appointment with the hangman at Wandsworth Jail on 6 August 1949.

John Reginald Halliday Christie

Even today, so long after the events, we still shudder when we hear of John Christie's monstrous crimes, both during and after the war. Born in 1898 near Halifax to a strict disciplinarian father and an over-protective mother, and the second son with four sisters, he was to become one of England's most shocking and prolific serial criminals, listing rape, necrophilia and murder amongst his repertoire. He was also directly responsible for sending an innocent man to the gallows.

Three events in his childhood are said to have shaped Christie's future conduct. Viewing the dead body of his grandfather at the age of eight is alleged to have fascinated him. He had been afraid of his grandfather in life but in death he held an allure that led to the young Christie being drawn to playing in the local cemetery, interested in the interred coffins there. At ten, his narrow Edwardian mind was shocked by a brief flash of his married sister's leg to the knee as she adjusted her shoe. At fifteen, kids being kids and cruel, he was taunted by contemporaries for his lack of sexual prowess while out on a group walk during which couples paired off in the local lover's lane. His partner told all and taunts of 'Can't-do-it-Christie' humiliated him, sowing the seeds of a powerful hatred for women.

At eighteen he enlisted in the army, where he was uncomplaining and cheerful. It was at this period of his life that he began to visit prostitutes; non-threatening and undemanding as he was their client.

He was gassed in June 1918 when a mustard shell exploded beside him and he was knocked unconscious, injuring his voice and, he claimed falsely, blinding him temporarily. He spoke in a whisper for the rest of his days, although this was psychologically induced. He received a disability pension on discharge from the military.

Christie married passive, unworldly Ethel Simpson Waddington at Halifax Register Office on 10 May 1920. For a time, they were happy, although it is said to have taken a while for the marriage to be consummated.

He was always happiest in a uniform and was a scout as a child, often wearing the uniform when not engaged on scouting activities. He subsequently worked in a number of jobs, including as a postman. Despite this seemingly happy home and work life, he began visiting prostitutes once more and was then sentenced to three months' imprisonment for stealing postal orders. Ethel stood by him but he was disowned by his family. Ethel's patience wore thin after he was bound over to keep the peace for obtaining money by false pretences and put on probation for twelve months for violent conduct in 1923. Christie walked out and went to London, where he was once again imprisoned, this time for larceny. He drifted, working where and when he could. In 1929, he was sentenced to six month's hard labour for hitting the prostitute with whom he lived over the head with a cricket bat, leaving a five inch wound. The magistrate called it, 'a murderous attack,' (Kennedy, 1961). In 1933, he was once again in trouble, this time for stealing a car from a Roman Catholic priest who had befriended him.

It was at this point that he decided that life was better with Ethel than without her and wrote to ask her to come back to him. She came and Christie made an effort at sorting his life out, obtaining work as a ledger clerk although, behind Ethel's back, he continued to visit prostitutes. In 1938, the couple moved to a small flat in 10 Rillington Place, a run-down property in Notting Hill, near Ladbrook Grove underground station. The stage was now set for the horrors to come.

With the war came a new uniform. Despite his criminal record, Christie was accepted as a special constable and delighted in the power that the uniform brought, winning awards for his 'ability relating to criminal offences' and obtaining a first aid certificate that he would misuse later. The uniform also opened the way for bribes and favours as he exploited the black out. Christie found this period of his life both lucrative and exciting – the job gave him access to the dead bodies that fascinated him as thousands were killed during bombing raids at the height of the London Blitz. Death was all around him. As Ludovic Kennedy observes, the four years he was a policeman in war torn London were, 'probably the happiest years of his life.'

However, in 1943, being caught in flagrante delicto by his lover's soldier husband, and badly beaten as a result, undermined his position and he was a bitter man. So bitter in fact, that he was pushed over the edge.

Ruth Fuerst

Ruth Fuerst, an Austrian who had escaped Hitler in 1939, became Christie's first known victim in August 1943. She was a part-time prostitute to make ends meet and the last time in Christie's bed was not the first time. Christie strangled Ruth with a rope while having intercourse with her. He then bundled her under the floorboards in the living room while he decided what to do with her body. Ethel had been away in Sheffield and returned bringing her brother with her to stay. Henry Waddington slept the night in the front room, just feet above Ruth's dead body. Ethel and Christie slept in the bed Ruth had been killed on. The next day Christie dug a grave in the garden and buried her, having burned her clothing.

Muriel Eady

Respectable Muriel lived with her aunt in Putney. When Christie left the police following the scandal in 1943, he joined the Ultra Radio Works in Acton. Muriel worked on the assembly line there. Christie invited Muriel and her gentleman friend to tea with himself and Ethel. The four got along well and met again, going to the cinema together. Christie planned his movements with precision and cultivated Muriel's trust, so that she was unsuspecting when Christie invited her to his home under the pretence of being able to cure her of catarrh with an inhalation device. She knew he had been a policeman and had medical knowledge, so trusted him. Thus, in October 1944 when Ethel was in Sheffield visiting her family, Muriel came to

Left: John Reginald Halliday Christie with his wife, Ethel. Christie abused trust to carry out a series of murders at 10, Rillington Place, including the wartime murders of Ruth Fuerst in 1943 and Muriel Eady in 1944. Both were strangled with what Christie called 'my strangling rope.' Ethel was to follow in 1952.

Rillington Place for Christie's 'cure'. After drinking tea, she inhaled deeply from a device with two tubes, one running Friar's Balsam and the other attached to a gas point. When the bulldog clip holding the gas back was released, Muriel was doomed. Incapable from the gas, Christie took her unresisting body to the bedroom and strangled her as he raped her. Muriel Eady was then buried in the garden, a short distance from Ruth Fuerst.

Both victims were reported missing but there was a war on. People were missing all over London, some resurfaced, others were not so lucky. Christie, literally, got away with murder.

For several years after the war, Christie lay low. He worked for the Post Office once more and respectability descended again on the household. That is, until 1948 brought new tenants to the top floor flat at 10 Rillington Place.

Timothy, Beryl and Geraldine Evans

Timothy John Evans was a compulsive liar, who was assessed as having a mental age of between ten and eleven, and the vocabulary of a fourteen-year-old (Marston, *John Christie* 2007). He had been in and out of hospitals for most of his childhood and so his education had been little and in widely spaced intervals. Spinning stories helped him to get through life. Little did he know that they would cost him dear. His wife, Beryl, had worked on the switchboard at Grosvenor House in Mayfair. They married on 20 September 1947. The couple moved into the two-roomed apartment at Easter. He was twenty-three and Beryl was nineteen. In October 1948, Beryl gave birth to a baby girl, Geraldine, and life was happy for the little family. They got on well with Christie and his wife and Beryl turned down the offer of a ground floor apartment with a garden because she liked living at Rillington Place so much.

However, Beryl found it difficult to adjust to life as a mother and Evans was out working long hours as a delivery man to try to make ends meet. They drifted into debt and rows ensued. When, in 1949, Beryl found she was pregnant for a second time, she was dismayed and looked for some way to abort the baby. Christie told her he had experience of such matters and offered to help. Her acceptance sealed her fate. Like a predatory shark, Christie had been biding his time, watching the pretty girl who lived upstairs. For him, her unwanted pregnancy was heaven-sent. While workmen were making repairs to the house and the elderly and blind tenant in the first floor flat was in hospital, it was the perfect time for Christie to plan his third murder. At lunchtime on Tuesday 8 November 1949, Evans reluctantly reconciled with the idea of a termination, Christie went up to the waiting Beryl. He laid her on a quilt in front of the fire and asked her to breathe from a tube from the gas tap. He continued the pretence of medically aborting her by trying to slip a spoon inside her vagina. When she struggled against the gas, he, by now sexually excited, hit her repeatedly until she stopped struggling. He then strangled her with what he called, "my strangling rope" (Kennedy) and had intercourse with her body. When Beryl's friend, Joan Vincent, knocked on the door of the little garret flat, it must have been an almost heart-stopping surprise for Christie. Beryl and Joan saw each other at lunch time several days a week and so Joan was upset to find that she could not open the kitchen door more than a little because someone was leaning against it from the inside. She went away and was to tell police later that she was 'so dreadfully upset' (Kennedy) by the incident, thinking that her friend was angry with her for some reason.

Timothy Evans came home to find his wife dead, battered and bloodstained. Christie made sure that Evans knew he was an accomplice to the death of his wife. Not wanting to implicate Christie, who, after all, had been trying to help the young couple, and in any case, in awe of the ex-policeman, Evans did not go to the police about Beryl's death. Instead, unable to think of a better plan, he helped Christie carry Beryl's body to the downstairs empty flat, from where Christie said he would dispose of it by throwing it down a drain.

Little Geraldine was the next problem to solve. What to do with her now her mother was not there to look after her and her father was out at work all day? A baby by itself would lead to questions being asked and invite discovery. Kindly Christie wanted to help and so told Evans that he knew of a couple in East Acton who would be glad to adopt the baby. He told Evans to say that both Beryl and little Geraldine had gone away on holiday to stay with Beryl's father in Brighton. This is the story that Evans gave when asked, further implicating himself in the process. When Evans went to work on 10 November, the day after Beryl's murder, he left Geraldine ready to go to her new home. It was the last time he was to see her. Although Christie never confessed to killing Geraldine, it is certain that it was he who strangled her, as he had her mother.

The easily-led Evans lost his job that day. He had been continually asking for advances of pay and his boss asked him what he wanted the money for. Evans repeated the lie that Christie had given him, saying that his wife and daughter were away on holiday, staying with family in Brighton, and he wanted to send them some cash. Christie further led Evans by suggesting that he sell up his furniture and move away to start afresh. This Evans did, selling the furniture for £40, although he had not finished paying for it, and going to stay with his aunt and uncle in Wales. This withdrawal was later to be seen as that of a murderer on the run, although, as Edward Marston (2007) points out, it was more a 'leisured withdrawal from a city that held too many sad memories.' In Wales, he repeated the story that Beryl and Geraldine were away and talked fondly of the baby, buying her a teddy-bear in Woolworths in Merthyr Tydfil.

Worry about Geraldine was to be his downfall. Evans returned to Rillington Place after six days. Christie would not give him the name and address of the couple he said had taken her. Instead, he said that she must be given two or three weeks to settle in. He did not invite Evans in and the two of them caught the same bus, Christie saying that he was on his way to visit his doctor. This information, when checked, proved to be a lie as there was no record of a visit from Christie that day. When Evans returned to Wales, his family started to get suspicious. He was borrowing money and enquiries made in Brighton had revealed that Beryl and the baby were not there. This meant that questions were being asked about the pair's whereabouts. Visits to Rillington Place led to contradictory reports of

With the trail clearly stopping at Rillington Place, the police now searched the house, failing to find any of the four bodies stashed there.

Beryl's leaving, with Ethel Christie stating that she and the baby had said goodbye on 8 November and promised to write. However, while Christie himself said that Beryl had walked out. Evan's mother, Thomasina Probert, had had to pay the outstanding finance for the furniture and was being chased for money owed by her son. In Wales, Evans was finding it hard to talk his way out of trouble and finally went to the police on Wednesday 30 November.

Still seeking to protect Christie, he made a statement to the effect that he had obtained pills to abort the baby, which had killed his wife. He then put her body down the drain outside the house. He was amazed when police told him that it took three people to take the lid off the manhole and that the drain was empty. Christie had lied to him.

Evans then made a second statement, this time mentioning the illegal abortion and Christie's part in it and in the disposal of the body. The police visited Mrs Probert, asking for the whereabouts of Beryl and Geraldine. Evans had asked her to visit Christie to get the address of the couple Geraldine was supposed to be living with. His mother admitted to the police that her son was a compulsive liar. With the trail clearly stopping at Rillington Place, the police now searched the house, failing to find any of the four bodies stashed there. They did not search the wash house, which is where they would have found Beryl and Geraldine. They found a stolen briefcase and so Evans was arrested for having taken it. Christie was interviewed at London's Notting Hill police station, where he proceeded to undermine anything that Evans might say. He was careful to present he and Ethel as a united, respectable front. Evans and his wife had argued a lot and Beryl was in fear of her life as a result, he reported, completely at ease in a police station. She was desperate to abort her second baby and he and

Ethel were concerned about her. Ethel would later tell police that Beryl's friend Joan Vincent had caused trouble in the household and that Beryl had hidden herself in the kitchen on that fateful day so as not to see her. Christie had schooled his wife well. Why Ethel lied remains to be seen. She must have been suspicious of her husband but followed his directions to mislead the police.

A further search of the house led to the wash room and the grim discovery of the bodies of both Beryl and Geraldine. Geraldine still had the tie that strangled her wound around her neck.

Evans was brought back to the capital very much as a guilty man, escorted by two burly police officers, despite having no criminal record. At the Notting Hill police station, he was shown two piles of clothing. One was Beryl's, complete with the blanket and sash cord she had been found wrapped and secured in. The other's was Geraldine's and included the tie that had killed her. When it was put to him that he had killed both his wife and his daughter, Evans said, "Yes." What was going through his mind we can only guess at. He was questioned over the next two nights and produced several confession statements that were contradictory and, if the police had not been sure of their man, would have been seen to be patently untrue. However, the police were certain they had got the man responsible for the murders and the case went to trial. Evans' solicitors, Messrs Freeborough, Clack and Co. did not interview any of the chief witnesses to the case: the workmen who were working at the house at the time of the murder and who were in and out of the wash room at the time Evans was supposed to have stashed his victims; Joan Vincent, Beryl's friend who had been so upset by Beryl's apparent unfriendliness when she called as usual on 8 November; Maureen, Evan's half-sister, who had had the contradictory conversation on the doorstep of 10 Rillington Place. They did no digging into Christie's criminal past. The legal aid-funded firm had clearly already decided guilt and were going through the motions.

The case came to court at the Old Bailey on 11 January 1950 and John Christie was the star witness. Evans was charged with the murder of his daughter but, because there was evidence to be presented that was about his wife, as Marston points out, he would effectively be charged with both murders, despite objections from his lead defence barrister, Malcolm Morris. Christie was a credible witness, making sure that his First and Second World War service did not go unnoticed. He told the jury about the rows coming from the top floor flat, the threats of murder and an ominous thud in the middle of the night. He also mentioned that on 8 November he was in bed, unable to rise due to enteritis and fibrositis. Morris was unable to shake Christie, even after bringing up his criminal record.

When Evans came into the witness box, he said that he had confessed because he was afraid of a police beating if he did not. He had been stunned by the news of the discovery of his baby's body. It was the police who had told him where the bodies had been found. Prosecution barrister Christmas Humphreys reduced Evans from a small man to a pathetic one. He confused him, made him sound dishonest and harangued him for accusing 'a perfectly innocent man', Christie, of the murders. In his closing speech, Morris, for the defence, presented a weak argument that was neither persuasive or memorable, in stark contrast to the prosecution's staunch insistence of guilt. In summing up, Mr Justice Lewis gave a long and biased speech, pointing out that Evans was a confirmed liar and asking the jury 'whether you accept Christie's evidence against this man or whether you accept this man against Christie' (Marston). The jury took just forty minutes to find Evans guilty of the murder of Geraldine Evans and he was sentenced to death. On leaving the court, Mrs Probert, Evans' mother, pointed to Christie and shouted, 'Murderer, murderer!' (Kennedy). Evans was hanged on 9 March 1950.

Ethel Christie

Christie lost his Post Office job because of the disclosures about this past in the court case. He was terrified that bones from the bodies buried in the garden would be discovered and the ownership of the house changed hands, with West Indian tenants now living in the run-down property. He visited his doctor complaining of depression. Eventually, he found another job, this time with the British Roads Service. However, over time his state of mind deteriorated and he was an in-patient at Springfield Mental Hospital in July 1952. Ethel, too, was now being treated for depression. Tensions with the new tenants and Christie's now complete impotence were the main causes. Christie suggested she go to stay with relatives but she refused, thus depriving him of the advantage of her absence. In December, Christie had had enough. He left his job and strangled his wife while she was in bed. She was fifty-four. He then left her in their bed for several days before depositing her body under the floorboards in the front room.

Rita Nelson

Christie seems finally to have tipped over the edge. Accounts of his actions after Ethel's murder read as of someone who has been unchained and moving towards an inevitable date with destiny. Now alone apart from family pets and so hard up that he forged his wife's signature to access her savings, he sold most of his furniture and looked around for more prey.

His next victim was a prostitute, working at a Lyons' Corner House. Rita Nelson met the same fate as his first two victims when she inhaled gas while sitting in Christie's deck chair. She was raped and strangled, despite being 24 weeks pregnant. She was then stuffed into an alcove in the kitchen. Nelson was reported missing by her landlady on 19 January 1953.

Kathleen Maloney

Alcoholic Maloney seems to have been a sad figure. She had been brought up in a convent as she was an orphan but had run away for a different life. That life turned out to be one of prostitution, drink and a swarm of illegitimate children.

During the second week of December 1952, Christie took nude photographs of one prostitute while the other, Maloney, watched. While Rita Nelson's landlady was fretting over the whereabouts of her tenant, Christie was getting ready for his next murder. He met Maloney in a pub, took her back to his flat and sat her in his favourite chair. She was befuddled by drink so it was an easy matter to subdue her enough to administer the gas, strangle her and have intercourse with her body. The next morning, she joined Rita Nelson in the alcove.

Hectorina Maclennan

Twenty-six-year-old Maclennan was his next victim, although he had tried to persuade catarrh sufferer Margaret Forrest to come to him for his 'cure'. She lost his address and did not turn up, an oversight that saved her life.

Maclennan, another prostitute, was looking for a flat in March 1953. Christie offered her his flat, which he said he was leaving because of a work move. She turned up to view it with her boyfriend, Alex Baker, an unemployed lorry driver. After spending three nights with Christie because they were locked out of their digs, Christie was determined to add Maclennan to his list of conquests. He went to the Labour Exchange when he knew that Baker would be there and managed to entice Maclennan back to his flat by herself. She told Baker she was going to Rillington Place. Clearly, Christie was now ready to take greater risks, regardless of the consequences. Maclennan became his next victim, despite trying to fight Christie off. She was gassed, strangled with the trusty rope and her body used as the others had been before her. She was then bundled unceremoniously into the alcove with the rest. When Baker came looking for Maclennan, Christie made him a cup of tea and then joined him in searching local streets looking for her. He also took to meeting Baker at the job centre to ask if there was any news of her.

The End

By now, there was a strange smell in the flat. The cause was not discovered until after Christie has absconded, having fraudulently sub-let his flat and

Above: After going on the run, Christie was recognised and detained by PC Thomas Ledger, on 31 March 1953. He had killed eight people and was directly responsible for the death sentence handed to Timothy Evans.

disappeared with advance rent to the sum of £7 13s. The tenant in the flat above came down into the kitchen to put up wall brackets and realised that there was a hollow space in the wall. He found Christie's alcove, complete with bodies. When the police searched the house and garden, the bodies of Maclennan, Maloney, Nelson and Ethel Christie were found and the bones of Fuerst and Eady were uncovered. An intense but short-lived manhunt commenced, with newspapers full of photographs and details of the monster at large. Christie, who had been living rough, was recognised and stopped by a beat constable, PC Thomas Ledger, near Putney Bridge on 31 March 1953.

When questioned, Christie frequently confused his victims. His explanation for so many dead women found in his home was often that he was helping them. His wife, for example, was having convulsions and was past help, so he 'put her to sleep' (Marston). Nelson's murder was self-defence after she attacked him. He did not mention the gas attacks or the sexual intercourse with his victims, which were both revealed by post mortem examinations. Explaining the death of Beryl Evans as assisted suicide because her husband was beating her, Christie said that he had convinced Evans that she had gassed herself. He loved life in Brixton jail while awaiting trial and took to discussing his case with admiring fellow inmates. He was careful not to say a word about the death of little Geraldine though. Cons might admire a lady-killer, but might not feel so charitable to a child murderer.

Christie was brought to trial on 22 June 1954 at the Old Bailey. The case was presided over by Mr Justice Finnemore. Microphones had to be installed so that Christie could be heard when he gave evidence. Fifty-four-year-old Christie pleaded guilty to murder on the grounds of insanity. His defence lawyer, Derek Curtis-Bennett QC, said that a 'defect of reason' (BBC) was at the heart of the murders. Christie knew what he was doing but not that it was wrong. The jury took one hour and twenty-two minutes to decide that this was rubbish and convicted him of the murder of his wife, Ethel. He was hanged at Pentonville Prison on 15 July 1953.

Aftermath

10 Rillington Place was pulled down with the rest of the street in the 1970s, after the film of the same name, starring Richard Attenborough as John Christie, was filmed there. The area is known now as Bartle Street.

Timothy Evans was granted a posthumous pardon in 1966.

Should Christie have been made a special constable at the outbreak of the war? He had several convictions, including one for a serious assault on a woman. If these had come to light would he have been appointed? Would he have gained the trust of respectable women like Muriel Eady and Beryl Evans if he had not been a policeman? The perceived trust that his wartime position gave him allowed him great control over his victims and he was undoubtedly seen as above suspicion at the trial of Timothy Evans. However, Christie was a calculating predator. It seems likely that, position of trust or not, he would have found a way to satisfy his urges.

Harry Dobkin

With war comes opportunity only the conditions of the era could create. For one unhappy man, these conditions provided the perfect time to rid himself of a thorn in his side once and for all.

Harry Dobkin was born in 1901 in London and worked in the cloth trade after leaving school, eventually having a variety of jobs including as a tailor and a cook. When war started, he became a fire-watcher for a firm of solicitors.

Harry and Rachel Dubinski were married in 1920. It was a marriage arranged through a traditional Jewish marriage broker but, just three days later, the couple parted. Nine months later, their son was born. Rachel was determined to make Harry pay for the upkeep of their child. Harry was equally determined to make collecting payment as difficult as possible for his wife. It was this strife that eventually led to murder. In 1923 Rachel succeeded in obtaining a court order for payment of maintenance of £1 a week, although this was later reduced to 10s, and Harry subsequently served several jail terms for flouting the order. Rachel also filed four summonses for assault by her husband but these came to nothing. Rachel took to accosting Harry in the street to try to shame him into paying. That Harry was deeply in arrears is demonstrated by the fact that she was still doing so twenty years later, when their son was a grown man. It was too much for Harry to bear and he had had enough, although there were rumours of blackmail, which surfaced when Dobkin was interviewed after Rachel's death.

The blackout was a perfect time for foul play and bombing raids left convenient piles of rubble. People were frequently lost in air raid attacks and never found, or found and quickly buried. There was a war on, the authorities were stretched to capacity and needs must. At least, this was what Harry Dobkin thought when trying to figure out how to end permanently the torment that was his wife's presence in his life and, most importantly, not get caught in the process.

The answer was simple: bury her in the rubble of a building that had been hit.

On July 17 1942, a workman made what he thought was a routine discovery while helping to demolish the badly damaged ruins of the Vauxhall Baptist Church in Vauxhall Road, Kennington. There had been several bodies found in the ruins. Some were from the chapel's old burial ground. There seemed no reason to suppose that the mummified body of a woman of between forty and fifty years of age found under a slab was anything other than what it seemed, one of the more than one hundred victims of the raid on 15 October 1940 when the chapel was hit, or an unfortunate disturbed from her grave by the upheaval around her. The police were called as was usual and the body was sent to Southwark mortuary, where it was examined by Police Pathologist Dr Keith Simpson. Molly Lefebure, known to Dr Simpson as simply, 'Miss L', called the Dobkin case, the 'case of a lifetime' because it was to change the course of forensic medicine.

Simpson noted that the head had been cut from the body and so suspected foul play. The corpse had also had both arms and legs severed, the lower jawbone was missing, part of the face had been removed and the bones were charred. Clearly all of this mutilation was designed to make identification of the victim difficult. At the site where the body was found, builders' or slake lime was found. It was this that had preserved the body. Dr Simpson later found a blood clot in the victim's voice box that indicated that she had been strangled. He also noted that she had a fibroid tumour. He estimated she had been dead between twelve and fifteen months.

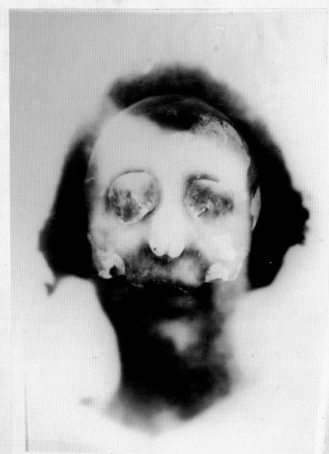

6

IDENTITY PROOF.

Superimposed full-faced
photography.

PLATE 6/7.

Single print from superimposition of Plate 6 upon enlargement
of Plate 7 to dimension as near same as possible without scale
or other means of establishing precise measurements of Plate 7

See General Report (No 2 - August 19. 1942.)

Above: Superimposed photo of Mrs Dobkin murdered by her husband in
November 1942. It was the first time that photography and science combined
to prove the identity of a murder victim (National Archives CRIM 1/1457 (6)).

The police, in the shape of Divisional Inspector FJ Hatton and Detective Inspector Keeling, whose work was later praised as 'brilliant' in the *Daily Mirror* (24 November 1942), checking the list of missing persons, found that the wife of the fire-watcher from the firm of solicitors next to the chapel had been missing for fifteen months. Rachel Dobkin fitted the description of the woman whose body had been found: between forty and fifty, greying hair, five feet one inch in height. Her sister, Polly Dubinski, also confirmed that Mrs Dobkin had had a fibrous tumour and gave investigators the address of her sister's dentist. This individual was able to give such detailed information, including the fact that she only had four teeth, three on one side and one on the other, that police could positively identify the body as belonging to Rachel Dobkin. Further, the head of the Photography Department at Guy's Hospital, Mary Newman, was able to super-impose a photograph of the skull on to a photograph of Rachel Dobkin. They were an exact fit. This use of photography was a first in forensic science.

Polly Dubinski had campaigned tirelessly to keep the police interested in her sister's disappearance. She had long suspected Harry of foul play. Polly and Rachel had visited a medium on 8 April 1941. The medium had foreseen Rachel going to a meeting and advised her not to go because she saw sadness ahead. Rachel promised not to attend but on Good Friday, 11 April, she met her husband in a café in Shoreditch, near to Harry's home. They left together at 6.30. It was the last time that anyone saw her alive. On 14 April, Polly again visited the medium and gave her a scarf and jumper belonging to Rachel. The medium went into a trace and clutched her throat, having a choking sensation. Both women went to another spiritualist and asked for her opinion. This medium also went into a trance and then announced, "There is a passing out, a sudden death." (*The Daily Mirror*, 24 November 1942)

On the following Monday, 14 April 1941, there was a fire in the cellar at the Vauxhall Baptist Church. It was seen by a passing police officer and reported at 3.23am. Fire fighters found Harry Dobkin at the scene, ostensibly trying to put out the fire. He admitted that he had been there for over an hour but had not called the fire brigade as he did not think it would spread. The fire was set deliberately, police believing that a straw mattress was used to start it. There was no evidence to link the fire to Dobkin and investigations were dropped. It is certain that Dobkin was using the fire to try to dispose of his wife's body.

Dobkin was interviewed about the disappearance of his wife, but, again, no evidence was found against him and so he continued on his way, free of his wife's constant pressure. Police made enquiries to try to find her whereabouts but eventually leads petered out and the trail ran cold. There was a war on and hundreds of people were missing.

With the discovery of Rachel's body came new suspicion about her husband and he was taken to the cellar where she was found. He denied all knowledge of the murder but was formally arrested even so. At his Old Bailey trial, he cut an unimpressive figure and failed to convince the jury that he was innocent. He was sentenced to hang and it was only after the guilty verdict that he confessed. He had been fed up with Rachel's constant demands for money. She was a thorn in his side that he wanted rid of. He met his date with destiny at Wandsworth prison on 7 January 1943.

Harry Dobkin took advantage of the wartime chaos and took a chance that his crime would be overlooked amidst the general carnage. He was unsuccessful but one wonders how many other murders were committed and the victims listed as casualties of war, rather than of murder?

Above: The Bellemoor Tavern, Southampton

The Worst Manslaughter

(with thanks to James Brown and the Hampshire Constabulary Historical Society for this story)

It was lucky that the Bellemoor Tavern, Hill Lane, Southampton had a telephone. Able Seaman Edward Thomas Lee, aged 26 and absent without leave from his base in Portsmouth, knocked on the tavern's door at 11.10 pm on 15 April 1942 and asked to use the phone. He called for the police and an ambulance as he had found a woman lying prone on The Common.

Lee, from Imperial Road, Shirley, met PS Edward Browne and, when asked where the woman was, blurted, "I killed her. She is Vera Bicknell who

Above: 'The worst manslaughter' – this image was taken from the edge of the footpath on Southampton Common, facing north. DC Jim Fibbens can just be seen, directly above the white arrow, about 160 feet away, waving a handkerchief and standing where the body of Vera Bicknell was found. **Inset above**: DC Jim Fibbens, who became Divisional Superintendent.

is 22 years old and lives at 45 Cannon Street, Shirley." He took the police officer to a point in some gorse bushes between Bellmor Gate and Pointout Gate, where the body was lying on the grass. Lee was taken to the Southampton Civic Centre police headquarters. The body was guarded overnight and taken for post mortem examination at the Western

Esplanade mortuary, by Dr James Webster, a Home Office pathologist. Dr Webster found that she had died from asphyxiation, caused by manual strangulation. She also had tuberculosis, which had collapsed her left lung and which would have made her breathless.

DI John Hill spoke to Lee, who subsequently made a written statement under caution in which he admitted killing the girl. He was married, with a small child and a pregnant wife. He had been seeing Miss Bicknell but his wife, Margaret, had refused him a divorce. His family, too, were not happy with the extra-marital relationship.

While on The Common on the fateful night, the pair had quarrelled about whether or not to finish the affair. She said that things were unpleasant for her at work because somebody had told her employer of the relationship. She wanted to end it. When he told her he had given up his wife and child for her, she had slapped his face. His temper rising, he remembered placing his hands around her throat, but nothing else.

He was medically examined by the senior police surgeon, Dr Grimston, who found recent scratches on his chest and right cheek. Lee was then charged with murder and replied, "I have nothing to say."

Vera Margaret Bicknell was born and lived with her parents at 45 Cannon Street. She was single and had been employed for the last year as a clerk at Toogoods & Sons, Seeds Merchants, in Millbrook Road, Southampton. Her family had been friends with Edward Lee and his wife for about ten years.

Lee appeared before Mr Justice Charles at Hampshire Assizes, Winchester on 17 July 1942 and pleaded not guilty to the charge of murder. His defence was led by Mr Alfred T Denning, KC, who had become King's Counsel in 1938 and was to become a judge in 1944. He was later renowned as Lord Denning, famous for his report on the 'Profumo Affair' political scandal in 1963, as Master of the Rolls and known as 'The People's Judge'.

Mr Denning did not dispute the facts of the case but brought evidence of Lee's good character in the Navy, having volunteered two days after war broke out. He sustained a head injury when his destroyer was blown up

Left: Vera Bicknell was buried in Hollybrook Cemetery on 23 April 1942 in plot K10/192. The headstone reads, *'In sweetest memories of Vera Margaret, the dearly beloved daughter of William & Lavinia Bricknell, who passed away April 15th 1942 in her 23rd year."*

and sunk during the evacuation of Crete and this had a steady and progressive deterioration in his mental state.

He called Surgeon Lieut-Commander Ross, R.N., who said that Lee had been under his care for some time, and that his frequent headaches, of which he complained, were due to his fear of service at sea. He was therefore suffering from an emotional disorder. When cross-examined he admitted that his mental condition 'was within normal limits'. The prosecution, led by Mr J. Trapnell, K.C., had already called Dr Thomas Christie, formerly Medical Officer of Broadmoor Criminal Lunatic Asylum and now Medical Officer of Winchester Prison, who said he had examined Lee on numerous occasions and could not find any sign of mental disease. In his opinion Lee would appreciate the nature and quality of the alleged act, also that what he was doing was wrong.

Mr Denning suggested to the jury that their verdict should be 'guilty but insane', or, as an alternative, guilty of manslaughter. At that point Mr Justice Charles shook his head, indicating that he did not agree.

At the conclusion of the evidence and speeches, Mr Justice Charles spoke at length in his summing up on the question of manslaughter. He said there was not a shred of evidence to support such a verdict and that it should never have been put to the jury. It was not in accordance with the facts or with the law and was put to them to divert them from the true facts, which were as plain as could be.

Here was a man, married, with a child and his wife now in child by him, carrying on an intrigue with a woman, obsessed sexually with her – it is a sordid dirty story, but we are not a court of morals. If a man caught a girl around the throat and strangled her, it was plain stark murder, and nothing else, unless it could be proved that the man was suffering from some disease of the mind and did not know the nature and quality of his act.

The jury left 35 minutes before the court rose for the luncheon adjournment, and returned after a total absence of one hour and a half. To the question "Do you find Lee guilty or not guilty of murder?" the foreman replied, "Guilty of manslaughter". There was a pause and the Judge commented, "I don't quite know what to say. I directed the jury that it was not open to them to find manslaughter. They have, in defiance of that direction and in falsity to their oaths, found that verdict. It is a verdict I must accept, although there was no evidence."

When DI Hill entered the box to give evidence of Lee's character, the Judge turned to the jury, which included three women, and said, "You can leave the box now; you are not fit to be here!" There is absolutely no question but that Mr Justice Charles was extremely annoyed.

DI Hill then said that Lee was born in Reading in 1916 and it was understood that when his father died in 1935 he was devastated. In 1935 he was engaged in the food trade in the Channel Islands. From 1937 to 1939 he was a tram conductor with Southampton Corporation and later as a labourer with a cable firm. He joined the Royal Navy on 16 December 1939.

At the time of the murder he was on his second marriage, to Margaret Dowding. They married in 1937.

Lee, who was in uniform, looked very white and stared straight in front when the Judge said, "The jury have thought it proper to find you guilty of manslaughter. It is the worst manslaughter I can conceive – you will go to penal servitude for 14 years."

Murder is never pretty but murder during wartime, when so much effort is being diverted to a greater struggle, seems obscene. Was it the extra pressure the war brought that prompted ordinary people to take a life? Or did the war give the mad, the bad and sad the impetus or means to kill?

Above: With a war on, any seemingly insignificant piece of information could be useful to the enemy.

In1942 it became illegal to do anything
with paper and card apart from light a fire
with it or give it to a recognized collector.
The penalty was a fine of £100 or three
months' imprisonment.

5

Fraud, Theft, Hooch, and Other Crimes

The Concise Oxford Dictionary defines the following terms as:
Fraud: **Noun** – criminal deception; the use of false representations to gain an unjust advantage
Theft: **Noun** – the act or an instance of stealing
Bootlegging: **Verb** – make, distribute or smuggle illicit goods (especially alcohol)
Treachery: **Noun** – violation of faith or trust; betrayal

From 1939 to 1945 the crime rate went up by an almost unbelievable fifty-seven per cent.

There seemed to be so many opportunities for dishonesty. There was always a doctor ready to sign a man as unfit for active service in exchange for a bribe. Those who were disabled could make a quick profit by attending medicals for the fit. After the Blitz, £500 was paid as an interim payment by the government to those who were bombed out and more was available to compensate for clothes and furniture lost in the carnage. Prostitutes carried on with their trade because no one would work with them and so, even if they did register for war work, it was difficult to find a job for them. Indeed, there were many ways that the unscrupulous could find to profit from the war.

There were also unforeseen areas that could lead the law-abiding to trip over. New laws cropped up all the time and keeping abreast of them was dizzying. For example, in March 1942 it became illegal to do anything with used paper and card apart from light a fire with it or give it to a recognized collector. The penalty for infringements of the new law were a fine of £100 or three months' imprisonment. In September 1942 it became illegal to dump rubber products in the household rubbish bin as every bit of rubber was needed for salvage. Absentmindedly dropping a punctured bicycle inner tube into the bin with the domestic waste could now land a householder with up to a £500 fine or two years' imprisonment, or both.

Felicity Goodall makes a perceptive point in her book, *Voices from the Home Front* (2004) when she says that much crime during the Second World War was a result of 'the population being starved of luxuries and in debt.' Many previously honest people were tempted off the straight and narrow because they were offered something they could not routinely obtain in ration-repressed Britain. With income tax at fifty per cent and inflation running at more than twelve per cent, the chance to help pay off debts was also too good to miss, with the rewards of white collar crimes such as fraud as lucrative as blue collar burglary. There was increasing unrest in the work place by workers worn down by wartime restrictions. The long hours, low pay and fear of losing their jobs all combined to hinder the overall war effort and breed the conditions necessary for the law-abiding to step over the line. In the meantime, at home, many landlords still demanded rent from the tenants of bombed out buildings.

White Collar Crime

A war often throws up unexpected ways that the criminally-minded can use to profit from the war effort. The regulations surrounding being bombed out were a case in point. The fact that, by 1941, there were some two million properties damaged or destroyed by enemy action and few staff to deal with claims for compensation, meant that the rules could be exploited by the unscrupulous with small risk of exposure. Officially, property owners, or those who held their houses on a long lease, had to wait until after the war was over to be able to claim compensation if their homes were destroyed. However, there was an interim payment available of £500 (£24,380 today), as well £50 (£2,438) for furniture and £20 (£975.40) for clothes. Those who wished to make a claim under the War Damage Bill (1940) went along to their Town Hall or council offices and completed Form VOW1. The compensation was not means tested and any one could claim if their home had been destroyed or damaged by an air raid. In addition, up to two years' worth of clothing coupons could also be claimed if clothing was destroyed. By December 1942, £86,500,000 had been paid out by the War Damage Commission for the more than two and a half million bombed out properties thus far (*Western Morning News*, 11 December 1942). With 60 million changes of address during the war years (Hodge, 2012), it is not surprising that it was difficult to keep track of claimants, particularly as there were relatively few staff at the National Assistance Office to investigate claims. This was the crack in the system that was exploited most often. The unscrupulous claimed multiple times for losses or claimed for damage that either had not taken place or was more minor than stated. Eventually, more staff were drafted in as the government realised that it was paying over the odds to get the country back on its feet.

Playing the system

One gentleman from Birmingham learnt how to play the system. Richard John Feakins and his wife Lyla May, both aged twenty-seven, from 127 Pershore Road, Birmingham, were brought up before the magistrates in Grantham in August 1941. Feakins was charged with stealing pyjamas, said to be worth 8s, and with two counts of obtaining money under false pretences. His wife was charged with stealing pyjamas worth 3s 11d. Claiming to have been bombed out, the pair and their child had stayed the night at the home of Florence Baxter, who had allowed them the use of the pyjamas, which belonged to family members. The couple then left the house early the next day, taking the garments with them.

From this relatively small offence there emerged the theft of £1 from Mrs Rose Lambley, whose husband was in the army. She had opened her service allowance envelope in front of Feakins, which contained £9 12s 6d. He had asked to borrow £1, saying that he could repay her when he received the £10 owing to him from a valuer following the bombing out of his greengrocery business in London. He had not repaid the loan.

Further, the Ministry of Labour were keen to prosecute Feakins and his wife because they had falsely claimed from the High Wycombe Assistance Board, saying that they had been bombed out. Feakins signed a claim form for war damage stating that their home, 47 Stafford Street, Stoke on Trent, had been damaged. They were awarded £4 5s but it was later found that no such address existed. The couple asked for several similar offences to be taken into consideration. Mrs Feakins was found not guilty and discharged but Feakins was sent to prison for two months for each charge.

Another case involved John Neal, aged 60. He was a debt collector in Hull earning 30s a week, who was sent to jail for three months for fraudulently claiming for war damage to a piano. He had already submitted a claim for £169 8s for clothing and furniture damaged beyond salvage but it was found that he was the seven-shillings-a-week tenant of an unfurnished room in the house that was damaged. He later sent in a supplementary claim for damage to a piano. In court, he admitted that he had never owned a piano and sent in the supplementary claim because he had not thought his original claim was large enough. He was not paid for either claim.

In Liverpool in 1944, four men were charged for claiming for compensation for war damage that was deemed to be a lack of maintenance. Building inspectors, suspicious of the claims made by property owner John

Mansergh investigated the work done at his property and found that it was not war damage but making good after neglect. Mansbergh was sentenced to twelve months' imprisonment and builder Walter Brisco to two years. Brisco's employee, Edward Dykins, and John Williams, Liverpool Corporation Clerk of Works, were cleared of involvement.

It could take years for investigators to catch up with those taking advantage of the war-time chaos. The *Lincolnshire Echo* of 7 February 1949, reports on the case of four Southampton men who had conspired to cheat the War Damage Commission by claiming for property between 1945 and 1948 that was either not damaged or had less damage than was claimed for. Investigations into questionable war damage claims were still ongoing at that time.

Clothing Coupon Crime

Buying clothing coupons on the black market was a simple way to add to the coupons allocated by the government, but with 700,000 coupons lost or stolen at the beginning of the scheme (Hodge, 2012) something had to be done to halt the tide or the whole system would fall apart. Black market clothing coupons were put a stop to by a government ruling that stated that previously detached coupons were invalid unless they were used for mail order clothing. Retailers then had to detach the coupon and stamp the book when making a sale.

Coupons were precious commodities and were often not returned when people died. Many people, it must be said, were too poor to buy new clothes anyway, despite regulated prices. Make do and mend was a way of life for the majority.

Utility clothing regulated the styles available for new clothing, whether made at home or by a tailor. The aim was to limit the amount of cloth used in the production of new clothes. By and large, the restrictions were accepted but in 1943 *The Times* had to print a *Warning to Tailors* for offences against the Making of Civilian Clothing (Restrictions) Orders, which were so rife that summonses were now to be issued. The main point of contention was the lack of a turn-up on gentlemen's trousers, which caused much unrest. Tailors had resorted to making trouser legs a little too long, so that customers could then use the extra length to make their own turn-ups.

Obscene Photographs

In an age where there are now differing degrees of porn and sex is portrayed on the television and in film in ever more graphic detail, the idea of an image that is merely 'obscene' seems a little quaint. Nevertheless, George Harry Cox and Eric Sheldon Haynes were busy supplying

Right: Pin up cards, sold primarily to servicemen, often trod a narrow path between acceptability and the downright pornographic.

'anatomical studies' they claimed had been 'passed by the authorities' (National Archives: CRIM 1/1297) to customers via mail order. They found themselves in court.

Cox was prosecuted for publishing obscene libels: On a day between 2 November 1938 and 8 January 1941 published 21 obscene libels to wit 21 obscene photographs.

Haynes was charged with procuring obscene libels with intent to publish and selling obscene libels: On 3 January 1941 sold four obscene libels to wit four obscene photographs.

The pair were caught in a police sting operation. The Metropolitan Police had received a parcel from Sidney William Richards, a civil servant, who had taken in the parcel for his son, a soldier. When he saw the contents, he went straight to the police. His son, Kenneth Sidney Richards, had sent the following order to Cox and Haynes on 16 August 1939:

> 6/- set of untouched anatomical studies preferably assorted male and female, failing this all female, age of model 20/21 years.

On 21 December 1940, Detective Inspector Ronald McDonald of New Scotland Yard, filled out a mail order form for four sample photos from Mssers Greenways, 27 Bond Street. He sent 10/- with the order, which he duly received on 4 January 1941. These premises were then raided and 2039 photographs were seized. Haynes, the proprietor of the photography business, claimed that his clients were 'mostly artists' and other responsible people.

Cox, a photographer for forty years, claimed the images were not indecent and that he photographed models and sold the photographs to Greenways.

At the Old Bailey, each was described as having 'a dirty mind' (*Birmingham Daily Gazette*, 30 April 1941). They were fined £30 each.

Careless talk

Other regulations governed the passing of information. It now became a criminal offence to pass on seemingly insignificant scraps of gossip. The *Daily Express* (13 May 1944), carries the story of Albert Edgar Coombes, who was fined £20 for careless talk. He worked for the telephone department of the Post Office and gave his wife some unspecified secret information. This she passed on to her mother who passed it on to a man later to find himself in the dock at a criminal court. When the information was traced back to Coombes, he found himself prosecuted under the Defence Regulations and was hauled before the court in Winchester. With a war on, any seemingly insignificant piece of information could be useful to the enemy and the authorities clamped down on transgressors.

".......but for Heaven's sake don't say I told you!"

CARELESS TALK COSTS LIVES

Right: Fifth columnists and spies were an ever-present menace.

Female criminals

Many of the crimes in this book were committed by men but it would be a mistake to think that it was only half the population who went off the straight and narrow. Two unlikely thieves, Kathleen Barbara Lawrence, a 21-year-old mannequin, and 19-year-old shop assistant, Maisie MacPherson, helped themselves to a typewriter belonging to Robert Lyndon Cutler in November 1940. Mr Cutler had closed his garage in Tangmere while he was away on active service. His wife visited occasionally to make sure that all was well, unaware that the two girls had their eyes on the premises. After taking the typewriter, they had then tried to sell it for 5s to a jeweller. When this deal fell through, they tossed the machine away. It was eventually found in a hedge. For breaking in and stealing the £7 machine, MacPherson, who had two previous convictions and had served three months in jail for stealing handbags, was sent to Borstal for three years by the judge at the West Sussex Quarter Sessions in Chichester. Lawrence was bound over to keep the peace for twelve months.

Shoplifting

'Mad' Frankie Fraser (1923 – 2014) was an East End gangster. In his autobiography, *Mad Frank and Friends*, written with James Morton, he explains how shoplifting in London worked during the war. Shoplifters were known as 'hoisters' and could, he claims, make £100 a week during the war by shoplifting to order. In the Elephant and Castle area was a long-established female shoplifting gang known as The Forty Thieves (also known as The Forty Elephants). During the war, the head of this gang was 'Diamond Annie', Alice Diamond. The gang had a long pedigree. It was well established by the 1870s and flourished until the 1950s. The members mainly stole clothes, which were then sold on very cheaply. Whole families were in the business. As Fraser admiringly points out, there were not the same numbers of shops as there are nowadays and the stores were quieter, so there was more chance of being spotted. The ladies had to return week after week and not get caught. The staff were long-serving and took their jobs seriously, so it showed skill, not to mention courage, to keep hoisting and not be spotted. If a gang member was caught, the penalty was severe. Fraser cites the case of his sister Eva, who was sentenced to six months in Holloway for her first offence of stealing a dress at the age of about seventeen, and of Joanie Fraser who was sentenced to penal servitude for three years for shoplifting soon after the war.

Roy Ingleton, in his book, *The Gentlemen at War, Policing Britain 1939-45* (1994), mentions the duties undertaken by women police constables during the war. Amongst several anecdotes illustrating that women were largely expected to escort women prisoners from one prison to another, is a short section about a case that Bristol policewomen had to investigate. Two black GIs helped two prostitutes to escape from hospital, where they were being treated for VD prior to being sentenced for soliciting. They then took the girls to a quarry cave near their barracks and made them cosy with food and clothing. The girls soon opened for business and it was the sight of a queue of black American servicemen lined up in the early hours of the morning that was noticed and which gave the Bristol policewomen something more than escort duty to do.

Ivor Novello

Ivor Novello (real name David Ivor Davies, 1893 – 1951) was a hugely popular Welsh composer and actor on both stage and screen. Novello's *Keep the Home Fires Burning* was a huge hit during the First World War and the Ivor Novello Appreciation Bureau calls him 'The Uncrowned King of British Musical Theatre.' The Ivor Novello Awards are given out annually to British musicians, composers and singers in his memory.

In 1944, Novello fell foul of the law for misuse of transport permits. When the case came to court, the gallery was full of the curious, eager to see the great man. The court heard that Novello had been refused permission to use his Rolls Royce car and was not happy about the decision. He had had the car converted from petrol to gas but was denied the licence from the Board of War Transport that would allow him to actually use the car. Regulations meant that only those vehicles that were essential were allowed on the roads.

He discussed the refusal of the licence with friends, one of whom was a fan, Miss Dora Constable, who had known Novello for several years and freely admitted to being infatuated with him. She worked for Electrical and General Industrial Trusts Ltd as a filing clerk. She offered to help her idol. Constable applied for the necessary permit, stating that the car was now owned and run by her company and was needed for vital transport between the company's various sites. The licence was granted. Novello was now free to use the car.

In reality, the company's managing director Charles Heyward, knew nothing about the Rolls Royce and Constable did not have the authority to make the arrangement. In court, Novello said that the whole idea was Constable's and he genuinely thought that the deal was real, despite never having spoken to any member of the company's management. Novello continued to pay for all the running costs of the vehicle, still kept it at home and paid for his chauffeur. Novello allegedly gave Constable a pair of his mother's earrings as a thank you gift for her assistance.

He was prosecuted and given an eight-week sentence, later reduced on appeal to 28 days, in Wormwood Scrubs, where he worked in the prison library. Prison was both a shock to his system, which he never really recovered from, and did his public image little good. However, the *Dundee Evening Telegraph* (3 June 1944) reported that there was much speculation about his release date and when he would return to the theatre. 'Fantastic prices' were being offered at the box office for tickets for shows in which he might make his first appearance on his release.

By prosecuting Novello, the authorities were making a statement. It did not matter who you were, if you flouted the law, you would pay. Members of the public did question the prison sentence though. A letter to the *Dundee Evening Telegraph* on 22 May 1944 pointed out that most people who had committed similar offences had been fined, not sent to jail. Novello never got over the shame of the prison sentence.

Borstal

Was it the ease with which crime could be committed that attracted the young or the adrenalin rush doing something wrong produced that was the attraction? In March 1945, four lads from Bournemouth were sent for trial at Surrey Quarter Sessions for breaking into a garage in Normandy, Surrey and stealing money and petrol coupons. The prosecuting barrister, Miss V Stephenson, called the behaviour of the youths an 'orgy of crime' (*Surrey Advertiser*, 24 March 1945). Two seventeen-year-old labourers, William Henry Seviour and Donald George Bromley, a seventeen-year-old tailor, Dennis William Lane, and lorry driver, twenty-one-year-old Derek Edwin Park, whose father was a police officer, toured the country in a variety of vehicles, which they stole as they went along. In Farnham, they stole a car wireless and accessories. All pleaded guilty. Lane asked for thirteen other offences to be taken into account and the others eleven offences each. All had previous convictions and were sent to Borstal.

A Lucky Escape

It was very easy to end up in court under wartime regulations and, as a consequence, the courts were busy. Sometimes, members of the public did not realise that they were committing an offence when they used what they thought was their common sense. However, during a war, common sense is not always lawful. A group of friends had a lucky escape after being caught flouting the petrol coupon regulations in Little Hampden, Buckinghamshire, in March 1944. Allan Walter Mills had tried to do his friends and family good turns when illness and vehicle breakdown disrupted the tidy flow of traffic in the area.

Little Hampden was remote and so permission had been granted for vehicles to be used for what, in more frequented spots, would have seemed trivial reasons. Doris Marjory Williams was able to use her car to take herself and a neighbour to the railway station so that they could get to work. Cecil David Batchelor could use his car to get to the station so he could go to work and also to take his son to school.

Williams was ill with pneumonia and so asked Mills if he would take her neighbour to the station for her, so that he was not inconvenienced. Mills agreed. To help pay for the extra petrol he was using, Williams gave Mills a petrol coupon for three gallons of fuel.

Mills and Batchelor had an arrangement to help cut down the amount of petrol used overall. They car-shared, with Mills driving Batchelor one day and Batchelor driving Mills the next. When Batchelor's car failed, Mills drove Batchelor each day. Mills gave him a petrol coupon to help pay for the extra petrol used.

Mills' father asked him to book a taxi for a visiting airman coming to the village. Mills forgot to telephone the booking through and remembered when the taxi office was closed. He knew where the owner of the taxi firm would be and so drove out to a dance being held in Great Missenden that evening. He intended meeting the owner there and making the booking for the next morning. However, he was stopped by the police at the dance, as it appeared to the officer that he had used the car for pleasure rather than as his permit to drive allowed. Mills then told the officer of the uses he had been putting the car to in Little Hampden. That the case came to be heard at the Missenden Petty Sessions on Monday 12 June 1944 (*Bucks Herald*, 16 June 1944) shows just how serious were the offenses that had been unwittingly committed. Mills was charged with unlawfully accepting petrol coupons which had been transferred otherwise than under the authority of a licence, and was summoned for both the acquisition and use of petrol. Williams and Batchelor were both summoned for each transferring a petrol coupon to Mills. All pleaded guilty.

Their defence stated that the petrol had been put to the prescribed use it had been licenced for, even Mills, who could use his car to shop, was, technically, buying a service when he went to find the taxi company owner to book the taxi for the airman. All had clean records. The verdict must have brought a sigh of relief to the trio. The case was dismissed under the Probation of Offenders Act, 1907.

This case demonstrates the depth of the regulations surrounding rationing and the use of petrol coupons during World War Two. It was the duty of the police to prosecute. These might sound like trivial offences, but set them into the wider context of the acute shortages of the time and they become much bigger. There was a set procedure for transferring petrol coupons from one person to another and if it had been followed, this case would not have come to court. Luckily for the trio, those sitting on the bench used their discretion.

Conman

Sometimes a practised conman could extract cash with a plausible story and a winning way. This was the case with Leslie Hunter, a miner, who had a way with words that allowed him to persuade Mrs Annie Shennan of 7 Balmoral Road, Dumfries, that he knew her sister, whereupon he was invited into the house for tea. He then told her that he was an Air Ministry Transport driver, driving a van that was short on fuel and he needed cash to fill it. He asked the good lady for £2, to be repaid immediately he arrived at his destination, so Mrs Shennan lent him 24s, which was all she had in her purse. It was the last she would hear of him until the police came knocking while they followed up leads to a string of other such cases. Hunter was convicted of theft and fraud and sent to jail for three months.

Ministry of Supply theft

The Ministry of Supply was set up in 1939 to coordinate the supply of equipment to all three armed forces. During the war, it was housed in Shell Mex House, in the Strand, London. The Ministry of Supply's reach was far

Above: Theft from warehouses, such as this food warehouse in September 1939, was immense. It was easy for staff to help themselves when they wished and organised gangs were adept at stealing to order.

and powerful. It built and ran the Royal Ordnance Factories; was responsible for supplying privately-built tanks and armoured vehicles; supplied labour to the factories and controlled research establishments. It was abolished in 1959.

Theft from the Ministry of Supply was a massive problem, both in wartime and post-war. The huge number of items that the ministry supplied was just too sweet for many people to resist, whether that be the petty pilferer, stealing for a small profit on the black market, or the larger thief, shopping to order.

James Rae, a worker in a Ministry of Supply munitions factory, helped himself to 1lb of explosive powder, valued at 8s, to make himself some gun cartridges. This, the Dumfries Sheriff's Court was told, was established procedure at the factory. The Sheriff was 'astounded' to hear that the workers thought they had the right to help themselves to whatever they wanted at the factory. He offered Rae a stark choice: a fine or imprisonment (*Dumfries and Galloway Standard*, 17 January 1942).

James Bowe, a Scottish labourer, found his way inside a Royal Navy armament depot and stole a 2lb high velocity shell case in January 1940. The shell case was produced as evidence at the Dunfermline Sheriff Court and the case against him was found proven. He was sentenced to ten days' imprisonment. How he managed to get into the depot was not addressed by the court. (*Fife Free Press and Kilkardy Guardian*, Saturday 13 January 1940).

Customers for stolen British arms and ammunition included Zionists in Palestine bent on rebelling against British rule. In September 1943, Lieb Sirking, a policeman, and taxi driver, Abraham Rachlin, were convicted of illegally buying looted British arms, being in possession of 300 rifles and 100,000 rounds of ammunition. They had been stolen by British troops in Egypt and smuggled into Palestine with the help of two members of the Royal Sussex and Royal Kent regiments, who were each later sentenced to fifteen years' penal servitude. Rachlin and Sirkin were leaders of the paramilitary Jewish Haganah, a defence force that, although illegal, had co-operated with the British during the war. They were sentenced to ten and seven years in prison respectively by a military court in Jerusalem. However, as part of a general amnesty, they were released in 1946.

The so-called Dead End Kids were a group of deserters in Egypt who befriended unsuspecting British troops and through them gained access to valuable supplies of weapons, food and fuel. Calling the number of such thefts 'appalling' RMP Major Crozier, explained that there were too few military policemen to deal with them (Charles Glass, 2013).

Meanwhile, at the West Riding Assizes, in March 1943, Albert Dalby was sentenced to eight months' imprisonment for stealing a rifle from a Leeds-based soldier and selling it on. His accomplice, Louis McMahon, a nineteen-year-old soldier, was bound over to keep the peace (*Yorkshire Post and Leeds Intelligencer*, Saturday 13 March 1943).

Post-war Surplus

Post-war, war surplus was big business for criminals. A garage proprietor in Coleford was sentenced to eighteen months in jail for receiving eight stolen Bedford lorry engines, stolen from the Air Ministry. It was not his first offence, having been previously fined for receiving stolen car timing chains. The prosecution alleged that the engines had been stolen to order (*Gloucester Citizen*, 24 June 1949).

John William Town, an East Kirkby miner, was fined £20, more than twice his annual salary, for stealing 200 woollen helmets and 60 pairs of seaboot stockings sent for reconditioning by the Ministry of Supply to a local hosiery firm and stored in their garage for lack of space elsewhere. Town sold the items on to colleagues at the Rufford Colliery (*Nottingham Evening Post*, 11 March 1948).

One man was charged with stealing 65,700 rounds of .22 ammunition and another with 64,700 from RAF Cottam in July 1948. They had entered the ammunition store and helped themselves. Two further thieves stole a motor car and motor cycles from the same base. (*Driffield Times*, 24 July 1948). That all these thefts were from one RAF site in a short space of time demonstrates how easy it was to take items. Donald Thomas cites the Report of the Comptroller and Auditor-General for 1945-6, which stated that listed thefts from the Army alone that year amounted to £20,000,000 annually, in real terms (*An Underworld at War*).

Thuggery and bullying

Air raid shelters were prime targets for petty crime such as pick pocketing or simply drinking a cup of tea and then walking off without paying for it. Felicity Goodall (2004) mentions the air raid shelters in Everton, Liverpool, which were taken over by gangs who would not let outsiders in. These bullies eventually got their comeuppance when local men banded together armed with coshes and went to visit the shelters in question. A few thugs ended up with headaches but the shelters were soon open to everyone once again.

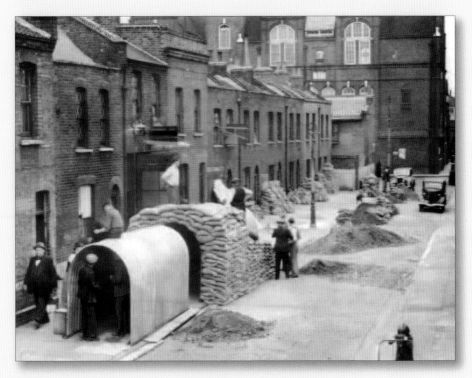

Above: Public air raid shelters being erected in the street in 1939.

Bootlegging

The 'world's most vicious drink' was how wartime bootlegged whisky was described in the *Newcastle Evening Chronicle* in January 1942. Since the First World War, duty on spirits had been high, prompting the rise in the number of illegal stills operating in Britain. Shortages of alcohol during the Second World War kept the stills in business and London, Glasgow, Liverpool, Leeds and Newcastle were particularly known as centres of bootlegged spirit production. Bootlegging, the unauthorised production of, often lethal, alcohol or other items, was rife and highly profitable. The poor quality spirit produced was often sold in the less reputable clubs and bars, where fewer questions were asked about its provenance and most of the punters were grateful for the opportunity to have something to drink at all.

The advent of US service personnel coming into Britain brought with them their slang, one term of which was 'hooch', a name for bootlegged spirits. In 1942, this caused problems amongst RAF officers and men in London to such an extent that the Air Ministry was beginning to wonder if RAF personnel were being specifically targeted. Hooch, a mixture of methylated spirit, wood alcohol, ethyl alcohol and water, caused tingling and numbness in the extremities, falling over akin to being drunk and sometimes permanent blindness. Apart from a slight odour, it was almost completely indistinguishable to first-quality alcohol and, decanted into a properly labelled bottle, the drinker would not be aware that they were consuming anything other than legal, legitimate spirits.

A bottle of what was described as 'gin' was passed to Herbert Morrison, the Home Secretary, for analysis. Mr Evelyn Walkden, the Labour MP for Doncaster, described the contents as 'fire water' and called for a clampdown on its production and sale. Nevertheless, as late as 1949, warnings about drinking hooch were still to be found in the press.

> **Hooch, a mixture of methylated spirit, wood alcohol, ethyl alcohol and water, caused tingling and numbness in the extremities, falling over akin to being drunk and sometimes permanent blindness.**

Espionage

David Leslie, in his investigation into doing time in Britain's toughest jails, *Banged Up* (2014), recounts the bungling attempt at espionage by thirty-nine-year-old marine engineer George Johnson Armstrong, also known by the surname Hope. The case was quietly but widely reported in the British newspapers. In November 1940, Nazi sympathiser Armstrong was in New

York on business that saw him meeting German nationals. Already on British watch lists as he had made no secret of his views, he wrote to the German Consul in Boston, Massachusetts, offering information and assistance. The letter was intercepted by American censors and he was arrested on his arrival back in Britain. Charged under the new Treachery Act with intent to help the enemy, his explanation for his actions was that he was trying to flush out German spies. He was found guilty at a speedy in-camera trial at the Old Bailey on 8 May 1941, by a jury of ten men and two women. His subsequent appeal was turned down on 24 June and he was hung at Wandsworth jail on 9 July 1941. Armstrong had the distinction of being the first Briton sentenced to death under the Treachery Act, 1940.

Beware of Strangers

Twenty-one-year-old Duncan Alexander Croall Scott-Ford was the Plymouth-born son of a Royal Navy veteran. He joined the Merchant Navy and found himself plying the high seas between Britain and neutral Lisbon. In Lisbon, he fell in love with a prostitute and this and his resulting desperation for money were to be his undoing. It would lead to his betrayal of his shipmates and his country. In a case that might have come from the imagination of a novelist, and which graphically illustrated how easy it was to fall into the hands of the enemy, a German spy approached him and promised him much-needed cash in exchange for information on Allied shipping movements. The man paid Scott-Ford 18,000 escudos, approximately £18, for his first report. This turned out to be all that he did receive and it was to be all that Scott-Ford's life was worth. It was only later that Scott-Ford realised that his folly had made him a target for blackmail. When he returned to Lisbon a second time, with more information for which he had been promised what newspapers called 'glittering prizes' (*Sunderland Daily Echo and Shipping Gazette*, Tuesday 3 November 1942), he was told that he had to keep supplying information or his assistance would be disclosed to the British authorities. Scott-Ford was neatly trapped. He had been seen with the German spy though and this was reported. When he arrived back in Britain, the hapless traitor was arrested. He was found to have in his possession memoranda relating to particular ships in convoys between Britain and Portugal, with details of their speed and course, and the aircraft guarding them. He gave a full statement, in which he admitted that he knew he was meeting enemy agents and that the information he was giving was at the request of the German spies. He also admitted that he had toured public houses looking for information from servicemen he met. Scott-Ford was charged under the Treachery Act, 1940. Found guilty, he was hanged at Wandsworth jail on 3 November, 1942.

Right: The British Free Corps was a unit of the Waffen SS recruited from British and British Dominion prisoners of war.

The Bravest Man

Albert Pierrepoint, the famed wartime executioner, called thirty-three-year-old John Amery the bravest man he had ever executed. He insisted on shaking hands with his executioner and told him that he had wanted to meet him, although, "not under these circumstances," (*Cornishman*, 26 September 1946). Amery, the son of the Conservative Secretary for India Leopold Charles Maurice Stennett Amery (1873 – 1955), was charged under the Treason Act, 1351 and convicted of eight counts of treason in November 1945, to which he had pleaded guilty. A committed fascist, Amery had moved to France in 1936 after being declared bankrupt in Britain. He travelled to Germany and subsequently made radio broadcasts supporting fascism. Hitler admired his views on a British volunteer force that subsequently became the British Free Corps, a Nazi-recruited unit of the Waffen SS consisting of British and British Dominion prisoners of war that was active between 1943 and 1945, and allowed him to visit prisoner of war camps to try to incite British prisoners to join the corps. Amery was arrested in Italy in April 1945 and was detained on arrival in Britain on 7 July. He was convicted on all eight counts at a swift trial at the Old Bailey after pleading guilty to all charges. It was later reported that he had wanted to spare his family the embarrassment of a long drawn out trial. Amery met Pierrepoint in Wandworth Prison on 19 December 1945. In 1946, there were questions raised in Parliament about Amery's mental state and whether he had actually been mentally fit to plead.

Lord Haw-Haw

This was the nickname given to Irish-American William Joyce, who held a British passport through his English mother, and who broadcast black propaganda to the British Isles with the drawling opening words, 'This is Germany (pronounced 'Jairmaney') calling.'

Joyce had been born in New York but the family moved to his father's native County Mayo, Ireland, when he was three. Here he was to witness at first hand the unpopularity of the union with the British. His family were Conservative and pro-union and suffered at the hands of the supporters of Sein Fein as a consequence. When Joyce was fifteen, the Anglo-Irish Treaty (1921) was signed and the family moved to Britain.

Two years later, when he was seventeen, Joyce joined the British Fascisti organisation. He was the leader of a group of fascists involved the following year in a brawl with left-wing agitators at a Conservative meeting in Lambeth. It was here that he received the long scar that ran down the side of his face that forever afterwards reminded him of his enemies, Jewish communists. Joyce left the party in 1925 and joined the Conservatives but left them shortly afterwards, disillusioned by the attitudes he found within the party.

Oswald Mosley set up the British Union of Fascists (BUF) in 1932 as an anti-communist political party. Joyce was quick to join up and very soon established his credentials by speaking and writing most effectively. He was also amongst the first to join in street battles when they occurred, often armed with knuckledusters. By 1934, the BUF had between 35,000 and 40,000 members, many of whom were disaffected Conservatives. William Joyce was then the party's deputy leader and later became its Propaganda Director. The BUF became the British Union of Fascists and National Socialists in 1936 and the British Union in 1937. The group, known as Black Shirts for the uniform its members wore, was anti-Semitic, adopted the Nazi salute and became increasingly radical, prompting violent clashes, including the infamous Battle of Cable Street in London in 1936. As a result of the repeated street clashes, the 1936 Public Order Act was passed, making it an offence to wear political uniforms, use threatening words and, for the first time, the Home Secretary was able to ban political marches.

Joyce narrowly lost the Shoreditch London County Council election. After arguing for ever more extreme stances on racial issues, Mosley sacked Joyce as Propaganda Director, fearing he was a threat to the party leadership. Joyce then joined the newly formed National Socialist League in 1938, with several other prominent members of the BUF. By the outbreak of war, the party was in decline and it was disbanded in 1940.

Joyce and his wife Margaret jumped ship and went to Germany in August 1939 for fear of internment in Britain, the fate of Oswald Mosley. He began working on German radio in September 1939 and became a naturalized

German citizen in 1940. His broadcasts sought to undermine British morale by showing that the British were losing the war. However, The *Daily Express* journalist, Jonah Barrington, who nicknamed him Lord Haw-Haw because of his exaggerated upper class accent, knew his audience. The name stuck. Six million listeners regularly tuned in to ridicule Joyce, although the element of danger – defying the government to listen to the enemy – was an added attraction and it went some way to reliving the boredom from the monotony of the official BBC broadcasts. However, he did cause consternation as some of his broadcasts were uncannily accurate.

Ultimately, Joyce moved to Hamburg as the Russian Red Army gained on Berlin. He made his last broadcast on 30 April 1945, signing off with a defiant 'Heil Hitler.'

He was captured near the German border with Denmark on 25 May 1945 and returned to Britain, whose government had hastily passed the Treason Act 1945 so as to have a basis in law to try him. Today, law students study the Joyce case. As Alex Softly points out (Heretical.com), despite being born in the United States of America, brought up in Ireland and being a German citizen, he was charged with Treason against Britain between the 3 September 1939 and 2 July 1940, the date his British passport expired. At a time when the country was still raw after six years of war, he was one visible public enemy who could be punished for his deeds. He was sentenced to death and was placed into the cell next to John Amery. Defiant to the end, he kept his appointment with the noose on 3 January 1946. He was thirty-nine years of age. His wife Margaret was interned in Sennelager, Germany, but never charged with an offence, despite also broadcasting from Germany and being known as Lady Haw-Haw. She was released in 1948. She settled in Hamburg and died in 1972.

Threat to National Security?

The *Daily Mail* of 1 April 1944 reported the verdict from the Old Bailey of the last prosecuted witch, Helen Duncan (1897 – 1956). She was a Scottish housewife, who worked part-time in a bleach factory. She was also a medium who helped to support her disabled husband and family by giving séances in spiritualist churches and family homes. She was so accurate that she caused ripples in the wartime establishment, who determined to put a stop to her activities.

In Portsmouth in 1941, Duncan held a séance during which a dead sailor from HMS Barham materialised and the ship's fate became known. The fact that the ship had been sunk by enemy fire had not been made public. One of the sitters at that séance wanted to verify what had happened and so called the Admiralty and the Home Office to ask if the sinking was true. He was told that it had happened as claimed and that it had not been made public knowledge because the news would shake public confidence.

This was not the first time that Duncan had been brought to the attention of the authorities. In Edinburgh, a similar event had happened after the sinking of HMS Hood during the Battle of Denmark Strait in May 1941. The news came through at a séance several hours before it was known at the Admiralty.

The Establishment was alarmed at the perceived threat to national security Duncan represented. She was arrested on 19 January 1944 during a séance at a chemist's shop in Copnor Road, Portsmouth, and charged with the only offence that the authorities could think of to prosecute her with, witchcraft, under the Witchcraft Act of 1735. She, and three others charged with her, were found guilty and she was sentenced to nine months in Holloway Prison. The outcome of the case was reported by the *Daily Mail* on 1 April 1944. There was such a strong feeling of public injustice at this sentence, that it was reported that her cell doors were left open while she was incarcerated. Duncan left prison vowing never to conduct a séance again.

Above: Helen Duncan, the last person to be prosecuted for witchcraft.

The Witchcraft Act (1735) was repealed and replaced by the Fraudulent Mediums Act in 1951. Duncan died five years later. Her family have long been campaigning for her pardon.

Crime, then, came from all directions and took many forms. For the unfortunate, it resulted in fines or prison and a shame that was lifelong. For the habitual criminal, the war offered all manner of opportunities and these were eagerly exploited, the possible consequences accepted as an occupational hazard.

Above: Shepton Mallet prison, built in 1610. The 1942 Visiting Forces Act allowed American Military Justice to be carried out on British soil. A new gallows was erected to execute American service personnel.

> ....there was a tendency to blame black soldiers and to scapegoat them for the crimes of their white counterparts. Thus, it was hoped that rape would be seen as a 'black' problem, rather than an 'American' one.

6

Armed Services Crime

The Concise Oxford Dictionary defines the following terms as:
Services: Noun – the armed forces
Crime: Noun – 1a: an offence punishable by law; **1b**: illegal acts as a whole; **2**: an evil act; **3**: a shameful act; **4**: a soldier's offence against military regulations

Crime was not just the preserve of criminal civilians. Conscription had scooped up men of all persuasions, criminal or otherwise, and they consequently found themselves in an unfamiliar arena, having to cope as well as they could. For some, this opened up new horizons, not always for the best. For others, ingrained prejudices were exported to new lands and added another dimension to service life.

American servicemen poured into Britain, bringing with them their gum, their confidence and a different mind-set – their country had a system of colour segregation that the British did not understand and which caused its own problems.

American Service Crime

According to the *Handbook on Sexual Violence*, (Brown, Jennifer M., and Sandra L. Walklate, eds, Routledge 2011), American GIs raped around 14,000 civilian women in England, France and Germany during the Second World War. This resulted in seventy American soldiers being executed for rape, murder or both. In France, where GI rapists were publicly hanged, there was a tendency to blame black soldiers and to scapegoat them for the crimes of their white counterparts. Thus, it was hoped that rape would be seen as a 'black' problem, rather than an 'American' one. 100,000 black American soldiers arrived in Britain during the Second World War. At the time, Britain's black population was only about 7,000 (BBC).

In Britain, part of the country's oldest jail, Shepton Mallet built in 1610, was taken over by the American government to be used as a military prison. A new brick extension was built and this housed a condemned cell and an execution room. A new British-style gallows was installed and the services of hangmen Albert Pierrepoint and his nephew Tom were commissioned. The 1942 Visiting Forces Act allowed American Military Justice to be carried out on British soil. Different sources give conflicting statistics for the numbers of executions carried out by the American military at Shepton Mallet, ranging from 18 to 21. Of these, two were executions by firing squad, the rest were hangings. At the time, murder in Britain carried a mandatory death sentence, rape did not but it was otherwise in American military law.

Looking at the available list of those Americans executed at Shepton Mallet is revealing. Nine were murderers, six were rapists and three were both. Ten were African American, three were Latino and five white. All were Private Soldiers, apart from one Corporal. American Courts Martial were usually swift affairs, often over in a day or two at most, although, to be fair, this was not particularly unusual for the time. The crimes make sorry reading.

Among those who met their end at Shepton Mallet was Pte David Cobb. He was twenty-one years of age on 12 March 1943, the date he became the first African American soldier to be hanged in the new execution facility at Shepton Mallet prison. He had shot and killed Second Lieutenant Robert J Cobner at Desborough Camp, Northamptonshire on 27 December 1942. A tired Cobb, he had been on guard duty, protested after being given a dressing down and Cobner ordered him arrested. In the ensuing scuffle, Cobb threatened the sergeant who tried to take him prisoner and then shot at Cobner when he intervened. The wound proved fatal and Cobb was charged with murder. His court martial, just a few days later on 6 January 1943, took less than a day. He was found guilty and received the mandatory death sentence, which was subsequently confirmed on review. He was duly hanged.

The case of rape and murder reported on in The *Western Daily Press* of 8 October 1943 was another of Shepton Mallet's American inmates. The newspaper gives details of the Court Martial of African American Pte Lee A Davis, aged twenty-two, who was charged with rape and murder. He had been out drinking and, in his own words, "… I was pretty intoxicated with beer, aspirin and Scotch …" He had stopped two friends returning from a trip to the cinema, Muriel Fawden aged twenty-two, a clerk at Savernake hospital, near Marlborough, Wiltshire and Cynthia June Lay, aged nineteen, a cook at the hospital. Meeting Davis terrified them into trying to flee. According to the Capital Punishment UK website, he is alleged to have said, "Stand still or I'll shoot." He forced the women into nearby bushes. Cynthia then tried to run, at which point Davis shot and killed her. He then raped Muriel, but did not kill her. This was his undoing, as she was later able to give police a statement. This led to all American rifles at the nearby barracks being inspected. Davis's had been fired. Later forensic tests linked shell cases found near Cynthia's body to the soldier's rifle. At the court martial on 6 October, Davis pleaded not guilty to murder and rape, saying that he had not meant to shoot at Cynthia, only fire over both girls' heads. Davis had scrawled an apology on his statement, 'to the girl in the hospital' – Muriel – that was read out at the court martial. He was convicted of both charges and hanged on 14 December 1943.

Pte Harold Smith had returned to his barracks in Chiseldon Camp, Swindon in January 1943, after a period enjoying the high life in London while being absent without leave. When he ran out of money he went back to camp, only to find that his unit had been moved on. Finding a loaded gun, he argued with another soldier, Pte Harry Jenkins and shot him dead. He made a dash for London and was there arrested by British police, who returned him to his superiors. Knowing that the game was up, Smith made a full confession and was found guilty of murder at his court martial in Bristol on 12 March 1943. He met his end at Shepton Mallet on 25 June 1943.

The rape of Dorothy Holmes led to the double hanging of Pte Eliga Brinson, from Tallahassee, Florida and Pte Willie Smith, of Birmingham, Alabama, on 11 August 1944. They had ambushed Dorothy and her boyfriend after they left a dance at Bishop's Cleeve, Gloucestershire. In the ensuing melee, Dorothy's boyfriend managed to escape and run for help. Unfortunately, that left Dorothy to her fate as she was dragged into a field and raped by both Brinson and Smith. Boot prints left at the scene were traced to the pair and led to their arrest. Their court martial was at Cheltenham on 28 April 1944.

Outcry

Not all cases of alleged rape ended in an execution. The case of black soldier Leroy Henry, from St Louis, caused an outcry amongst local people in the village of Combe Down. A married white woman with whom he had been having an affair accused Henry of rape. Her husband knew of, and did nothing to stop, the relationship, presumably because the money Henry paid his wife was useful. It was after Henry had refused to pay that the rape charge was made. Locals were incensed that Henry had been beaten while in military police custody and they tended to believe his story that the rape was a fabrication, concocted after his refusal to pay any further cash. More than 33,000 people signed a petition to stop the hanging. This was sent to the American General Dwight D Eisenhower, who granted the soldier a reprieve.

Attacked

In Somerset, one munitions worker noted in her diary for November 1942 that one of the girls working at the factory had been attacked and knocked into a hedge by an American GI who told her not to scream or he would 'knock your head off.' The girl was able to escape, shaken but unhurt and the soldier was later arrested. (Goodall)

The New Forest

Kenneth Robin Hood, the son of the police officer in Cadnam in the New Forest, remembered one job his father had during World War Two: dealing with the regular bar fights between servicemen and civilians in the local pubs (John Leete, *The New Forest at War*).

Patton

General George Patton, the leader of the Third United States Army in Europe, lodged for a while at Breamore House in the New Forest in 1942 and many of his troops were stationed nearby. A larger than life figure, he was always armed, the ivory handled pistols in his belt clearly visible, and he loved speed. His army loved it, too. American GIs, used to the wide-open roads of their homeland, did not always appreciate that the twisty, narrow byways of Britain were necessarily slower routes than they were used to. There is anecdotal evidence of New Forest ponies being knocked down by speeding American servicemen.

Sir Edward Hulse, 10th Baronet, whose family home is Breamore House, was born in 1932. He remembers Patton as a 'very physical man' who drove as if he was racing around the village. It is Sir Edward who also mentions the death of the publican's daughter from the Horse and Groom at Woodgreen, in a driving accident, hit by a fast moving American driver. The incident was, he says, 'swept away,' (*The New Forest at War*). As the New Forest Life website explains, incidents like this were perceived to be 'brushed under the carpet.'

The Canadian Riots: 'It was too much fun!'

This was the reason for disobeying orders that one Canadian soldier gave at his court martial for rioting in 1945.

The military town of Aldershot in Hampshire was the base for the Canadian Forces Overseas from 1939. There had been Canadian contingents in the town until 1920, the first having arrived in 1897 for Queen Victoria's diamond jubilee, so the local townsfolk were well used to their being in the area.

The First Canadian Infantry Division arrived in Aldershot in late 1939 and early 1940. They moved into barracks that had been vacant since the

ANGRY CANADIAN SOLDIERS WRECK ALDERSHOT SHOPS

ORGY OF SENSELESS DESTRUCTION IN SHOPPING CENTRE

Above: 500 Canadian soldiers rioted in Aldershot on the evenings of 4 and 5 July 1945. Headline from the *Aldershot News & Military Gazette*, 13 July 1945.

British First and Second Divisions had left for France in the previous September. That winter was a bleak one. The barracks were cold and damp, and came as a shock to the Canadian troops who were used to the chill but not the wet British climate. Many of the troops were soon ill as a result of the conditions.

The Second Canadian Infantry Division arrived in the summer of 1940, by which time conditions at the barracks had improved. 56,000 Canadian troops were then stationed in Britain. They became the Canadian Corps on Christmas Day 1940. This contingent grew as further troops were sent over in the coming months and, after the arrival of three more divisions and two tank brigades, the Second Canadian Corps was formed. They became part of the First Canadian Army, which fought with the British Second Army in the NW Europe Campaign as part of the 21 Army Group, commanded by Field Marshall Montgomery.

Aldershot was first a training establishment and then, as Canadian training at home improved, became a reinforcement barracks. To cope with the huge numbers of arrivals, hutted camps were built in areas around Aldershot and local premises were commandeered as hospitals or store depots.

Relations with the local population were good. Canadians married local girls, laid on birthday parties for fun-starved local children and many men stayed on in Britain after the war.

It was not until the war in Europe was over that this happy state of affairs started to change. Aldershot became a repatriation barracks as thousands of troops flooded back to Britain from the war-torn battle arenas in Europe. There, they waited to be sent home. They waited … and they waited. As SJ Anglim states in his article *The Aldershot Riots of 1945*, the 'problem was to obtain shipping for the return of troops to Canada while meeting the demands of the war, which still had to be won in the Far East.'

The incoming troops simply had to wait for their ride home. 400,000 Canadian troops passed through Aldershot in June and July 1945. Some had volunteered for service in the Far East, in the hope that the war there would be over before they arrived in Canada en route. The Canadians began to fret at the delay leaving.

The troops had been living on adrenaline while in the thick of fighting for three years. The bungled raid on Dieppe on 9 August 1942 had been a bloody battle for the Canadian soldiers, when they lost 807 of their contingent....

The troops had been living on adrenaline while in the thick of fighting for three years. The bungled raid on Dieppe on 9 August 1942 had been a bloody battle for the Canadian soldiers, when they lost 807 of their contingent, with another 1874 taken prisoner. In Sicily, on 10 July 1943, they played a decisive part in the taking of the towns of Regalbuto and Adrano, which led to the unhinging of the German defensive line in the north of the island. In the Italian Campaign they were involved in some of the hardest fighting and the Canadian Third Division assaulted Juno Beach on D-Day before being joined by other Canadian units in the invasion of Normandy. In 1945, these courageous veterans found themselves penned in, with poor pay and food, and little to do. As Anglim explains, 'Owing to demobilisation, the Repat Units were 200 cooks understrength and the Canadians' rations were poorer in both quantity and quality than those of their British counterparts ...' Discontent and boredom set in, despite attempts to provide training for life in Civvy Street when back in Canada. To add insult to this, local shopkeepers and the landlords of public houses cashed in on the Canadians' lack of understanding of the local currency and fleeced them unmercifully. Mark Maclay, in *Aldershot's Canadians In Love and War – 1939-45* (1997) noted that one example of this was a luckless Canadian squaddie, who had tendered a £1 note to pay for a cup of tea in a café, and received sixpence (2½p) in change!

Joy at the imminent return home soon gave way to impatience, resentment and unrest. In June 1945, there was a rise in the number of petty offences committed by Canadian soldiers. These offences were starting to escalate as the month wore on. Anglim mentions that on 21 June teenage Canadian soldiers were convicted of robbing a taxi driver and stealing his car. On 1 July the trial started of a Canadian soldier who had attempted to rape an Aldershot girl.

On 4 July 1945, a large group of Canadian soldiers met on Hospital Hill for what the *Aldershot News* later called an 'indignation meeting,' (6 July 1945). A rumour spread that there were three Canadian soldiers being held

Above: A large group of soldiers met on Hospital Hill on 4 July 1945, before marching into Aldershot and rioting.

in custody at Aldershot police station. This rumour was later allegedly traced to a West Indian private, L A States, who was serving in the Pioneer Corps. Despite pleas to disperse from a senior officer, a mob of over five hundred Canadians converged on the police station in support of their comrades. As they approached, along Union Street, Wellington Street and Victoria Road, they smashed the windows of businesses they passed. In Union Street, the amusement arcade fared particularly badly, with machines dumped in the street in addition to the damage to the windows. A senior Canadian officer finally diffused the situation, by showing a three-man delegation that the cells were empty. After damaging twenty-five shops and eighty-seven windows, the mob quietly returned to barracks. No one had been hurt and there had been no looting or drunkenness, however, the precedent was set.

The Canadian authorities agreed with local police that the problem was a Canadian one and they would deal with it. Extra military police (Provosts) were drafted in to keep order and the following evening Canadian officers patrolled Aldershot in vans fitted with loud speakers. Major General DC Spry, the senior Canadian officer in the area, spoke to the men about their grievances and promised to mend what he could.

On the evening of 5 July, a large mob once again formed, this time gathering in Prince's Garden. The frustrated Canadians marched on Union Street, smashing those windows not damaged the night before. They threw bricks and stones at passing cars. Shopkeepers trying to defend their properties were faced with threats of violence and, on one occasion, a gun was drawn. At the police station, an officer tried to speak to them via his loud speaker but it was faulty and only garbled sounds could be heard. The rioters jeered and moved on, bent on more destruction. The Canadian Military Police clamped down harshly, reportedly replacing their truncheons with bottles at one point (*Aldershot News*, 13 July 1945).

At the end of the two days of rioting, not a single thing had been looted and only £20 had gone missing. Aldershot town centre though counted the cost of the build-up of resentment within the Canadian troops: 200 shops had been targeted, causing £15,000 worth of damage. There were no further riots. Courts martial later sentenced over 100 Canadian soldiers for riot offences, sending five to jail. In his letter of apology to the Aldershot Borough Council, a red-faced General Montague, the senior Canadian officer in Britain, condemned, 'this small, irresponsible group of Canadian soldiers.' Finding replacement glass for the 22,000 square feet of windows broken was to prove embarrassing, too. A request for glass to be sent to

Above: Union Street, Aldershot, today. On 4 July 1945, soldiers rioted along Union Street, Wellington Street and Victoria Street, smashing shop windows as they went.

Aldershot from Canada was met with the information that all Canadian glass came from the firm of Pilkington in the UK! A shipment was diverted to the town to replace the broken windows there.

Although the Canadian force had made its feelings felt, there was, apparently, no lingering animosity. Aldershot Borough Council later decided to award the Canadian Army Overseas the Freedom of the Borough, which was presented on 26 September 1945.

Deserters

Deserters from a conscript army were inevitable. Charles Glass, in his book looking at deserters during World War Two, (*Deserter, the last untold story of the Second World War,*, 2013) states that there were 100,000 British troops and 50,000 American soldiers who deserted during the war. Glass marvelled that there were so few. In contrast, in the eleven-month period that the Americans were in Northwest Europe, Hitler executed 50,000 German soldiers for cowardice or desertion (Ambrose, 1997). Reasons for deserting were many, complex and often not understood, even by the deserter himself. Some were simply afraid and so walked away from the nightmare that was battle on the front line. Others were crooks and thought that they could earn a better, and safer, living by stealing military supplies and selling them on. Some were battle-hardened veterans who had simply had enough. The American Army had the death penalty as the ultimate punishment for desertion, although only one GI Joe was actually shot for deserting, Pte Eddie Slovik, for deserting in France, in 1944. During World War One, the British executed its deserters, its cowards, those who fell asleep on duty and those who struck an officer. By World War Two, the only crime that was punishable by death was mutiny.

George Orwell on Murder

George Orwell, in his essay *Decline of the English Murder (Shooting an Elephant and other essays,* 1950) laments that murder is no longer memorable, in the way that the crimes of Jack the Ripper, Dr Crippen et al are remembered. He analyses nine murder cases and concludes that eight of the ten criminals involved were middle class, six were cases of poisoning and seven involved sex as a motive. The object of most was to obtain a, usually small, amount of money from an insurance policy or some such. There was normally some sort of sensationalism involved: he cites Crippen's flight across the Atlantic with his mistress dressed as a boy, as one example. The tabloid-reading public expect, Orwell says, a certain type of murderer: a small professional man, a dentist or lawyer, living respectably in the suburbs in a semi-detached house that allows the next-door neighbours to hear suspicious noises through the party wall. He would have some position of authority within a local committee and would be led astray by his passion for his secretary or another man's wife. He would wrestle with his conscious before planning the murder down to the last detail, probably with poison, making only one small mistake that would be his downfall. Thus, Orwell summed up the quintessentially English murder. He lamented that few crimes would be remembered as these were because the method of murder was changing. All would be forgotten, apart from the so-called Cleft Chin Murder, which Orwell called a cause célèbre of the time.

The Cleft Chin Murder

In 1944, a mercifully short crime wave shocked the nation. The media, looking for a hook to hang their headlines on, dubbed the culmination of the wave, the murder of a private-hire cab driver, George Edward Heath, 'The Cleft Chin Murder' due to the substantial dent in the victim's chin. The case was to provide sensational fodder for both the quality press and the tabloids for the next six months.

Why was there so much interest in the case? As C E Bechhofer Roberts points out, (*The Trial of Jones and Hulten*, 1945) the case bore enough elements to keep the country 'agog.' The victim was rumoured to have black market connections; his discoloured fingers had prompted some newspapers to dub the case the 'Inky Fingers Murder' when the body was first found, and the prominent cleft chin was remarkable. In addition, the murderer was said to have links with Chicago's gangster fraternity and his accomplice was an out-of-work strip tease artist, who dreamed of becoming a 'gun moll' (Bechhofer Roberts). At the trial, history was made when a woman barrister, Mrs Lloyd Lane, was appointed to the defence team of a major case for the first time. The whole was enough to titillate the public throughout the investigation and trial.

It took the police a matter of days to piece the scene together and catch the culprits. The trail led to latter-day Bonnie and Clyde, Elizabeth Maud Jones and Karl Gustav Hulten. Hulten was twenty-two, married, Swedish-born and on the run after deserting from the US Army six weeks previously. He claimed to be an army officer and a Chicago gangster. Both claims were untrue. He lived in Boston, Massachusetts, and had enlisted as a paratrooper after the Japanese attack on Pearl Harbour. The US Army waived its right to try Hulten and, instead, let him be prosecuted with Jones in a British court. Jones was an eighteen-year-old former approved school pupil, variously described as a waitress, strip tease artist and a dancer, born in Neath, Wales but then living in Hammersmith. Her husband, from whom she was separated, was overseas. She dreamed of excitement.

The pair met in a tearoom on Hammersmith Broadway on 3 October 1944 and immediately stepped into a fantasy world. He told her he was an

American officer named Richard 'Ricky' Allen and she gave him her stage name, Georgina Grayson. While out for a ride in a stolen army lorry, she told him she wanted to do something dangerous, whereupon he made the claim that he was a Chicago gangster and the leader of a London gang. He showed her his gun to prove his tough-guy credentials.

In the six days of their relationship, Jones got the excitement she craved. The pair knocked over a nurse as she was cycling along a country road and then robbed her. They picked up a hitchhiker, knocked her unconscious and robbed her, too. They then threw her into a river in the hope that she would drown. Fortunately for the hitchhiker, she survived this ordeal. The pair's activities culminated in the murder of thirty-four-year-old George Heath, a married father of two from Ewell, on 6 October.

Hulten and Jones went out that evening with the intention of hailing a taxi and of robbing its driver. Jones stopped Heath's private hire car, both got in and they agreed to a hefty fare of 10s for a ride from Hammersmith Road, opposite Cadby Hall, the home of the mighty J Lyons Ltd., to King Street, a distance of a little over a mile. Jones, testifying at their trial at the Old Bailey in January 1945, in a voice so quiet that the judge had to ask her to repeat her answers several times as he could not hear them, said that between them they had only 29s 3d and had no intention of paying the quoted fare.

Above: 18 year-old strip-tease dancer, Elizabeth Maud Jones.

The driver, Heath, was himself something of a dubious character. As a private hire driver, he was not supposed to be touting for business or picking up passengers who hailed him, yet here he was doing both, and charging over the odds for his services. He had been invalided out of the army after Dunkirk and had moved his family from Battersea after their home had been razed on a bombing raid. It was rumoured that he was involved in illegal gambling and, at the time of his murder, he was awaiting a court appearance for assaulting a publican (Linda Jackson, Epsom and Ewell History Explorer website, 2013).

When Heath pulled in to the side of the Great West Road, as Hulten requested, Jones, sitting in the back beside the American, saw that Hulten had his pistol cocked and ready to use. She said in her statement that she thought he was going to frighten the driver with it, so that he could rob him. However, when Heath leant across to open the passenger door, Hulten, seated behind him, fired at him while he was off guard. The sound of the automatic pistol firing was heard over seventy yards away by the night watchman at Hudson Motors Ltd., William Hollis. He later testified that the 'muffled sound' he heard was like that of a heavy calibre gun fired in a confined space. The shot, Jones told the court, deafened her in the right ear for several minutes. Heath was shot in the back, a shot that, according to the pathologist at the inquest, Mr Robert Donald Teare, would have first paralysed the victim and then killed him within a quarter of an hour. Jones took those fifteen minutes to search Mr Heath and relieve him of his money, about £5 in notes and change, and small items such as a fountain pen and his watch. The taxi driver was found dead in a ditch in Knowle Green, near Staines, Middlesex. Hulten and Jones frittered away the money they took from Heath at the dog-racing track the next day. Hulten kept Heath's car, a V8 Ford, after abandoning the army truck he had previously stolen. It was this car that he used to drive around the streets in later, on the lookout for the owner of a suitable fur coat, after Jones announced that she wanted one. Hulten attacked a woman on the pavement, to snatch her coat. This was his undoing as, although he managed to escape police capture, he roared off in the stolen murder victim's car, registration number RD8955. This was, ultimately, what was used to trace and catch him. Police found the car parked outside Jones' home on 10 October. When Hulten came out of the property, he was asked if he owned the car. When he did not reply, he was arrested and found to be carrying a fully loaded Remington automatic pistol in his pocket, with the safety catch off. Jones, who gave Hulten an alibi for the day of the murder, subsequently went to the police and confessed all, in a bid to ease her conscience. Each implicated the other at their trial. Jones repeatedly said that she was frightened of Hulten and was intimidated into doing his bidding. Hulten said that he had wanted to go for a walk and it was Jones who had wanted to hail the cab and rob the driver. During Hulten's cross-examination by Mr J D Casswell KC, for Jones' defence, there was an elaborate examination of the murder weapon, designed to show that it was impossible to have armed it ready for use accidentally. Hulten claimed not to know that it was cocked and ready while stashed in the belt of his trousers, and that the 'jauncing' (bouncing) of the car had made it fall out of this position. Thus, his contention was that he did not know it was ready to fire when he had it in his hand with his finger on the trigger as Mr Heath pulled the car over and leant across to open the nearside passenger door for Jones to get out. After the shooting, Hulten displayed neither interest in or care for the victim.

After just eighteen minutes of deliberation, both defendants were found guilty of murdering Mr Heath. Information on the previous crimes confessed to was withheld from the jury until after the verdict was given.

They were both sentenced to hang. The newspapers at the time carried updates on the case and whether or not they would receive reprieves. A plea for clemency for Hulten arrived from America via the American Ambassador in London but to no avail. Hulton met his end at Pentonville Prison on 8 March 1945. Jones, who the jury had recommended for mercy, was controversially reprieved. Many people thought that she too should hang because, in war-torn Britain where everyone should be pulling together, the crimes were seen as cowardly. She was released from jail in May 1954. Ever the showgirl, later that year, she published her version of events, serialised in the *Sunday Dispatch*.

> **After just eighteen minutes of deliberation, both defendants were found guilty of murdering Mr Heath.... They were both sentenced to hang.**

Conscription

Conscription gave the youth of the day an education that most could not have foreseen as useful in civilian life. Some conscripts though, found that the skills they were taught and the access to restricted materials they were given combined to offer a heaven-sent opportunity.

The Bath Chair Murder

By all accounts, Archibald Brown was a tartar. He had served in the First World War; still referred to in 1943 as The Great War, and had become a miller by trade afterwards. He had had the misfortune to suffer serious injury in a motorcycle accident at the age of 24 and now, at 47, he was bitter, constantly in pain, unable to walk and was cared for by a trio of nurses. He had not, though, lost his wits and these he used to keep his family on their toes every minute they were awake. If he was not forbidding his wife, Doris, to see her mother, he was ringing the ever-present bell to summon her to his side to sort out trivial errors, such as flowers out of place in a vase (Feather, *The Rayleigh Bath Chair Murder*). His son Eric grew up used to beatings and humiliation.

The family lived in Rayleigh, Essex, at 'Summerfield' 19 London Hill. Rayleigh is mentioned in the Domesday Book and archaeological finds there have been dated to Roman and Saxon times. The area has a long history, the forests nearby being royal hunting grounds during the medieval era. The fact that it is only 32 miles from central London and is near to the coast makes it a convenient place to live.

Eric, having what today would probably be called a disturbed childhood, found adult life hard. He had been removed from his local school and sent to boarding school because his mood swings were difficult to deal with. He had been asked to resign from his job at Barclays Bank in Rochford, a position he had held from 1940 to 1942, because of his strange behaviour. He was called up at the age of nineteen and found himself as Private Eric James Brown in the Suffolk Regiment, stationed at Spilsbury in Lincolnshire. On 23 July 1943, Eric was home on compassionate leave and Archibald was as domineering as ever.

Archibald liked to go out every day in his bath chair and increasingly enjoyed the company of one of his carers, Nurse Mitchell. On this day, she had gone along to the nearby air raid shelter, where Archibald's Bath chair was kept, and had found the shelter locked from the inside. Baffled, she had sought out Mrs Brown and the pair returned to the shelter in time to see an evasive Eric emerge from the building. The two women pulled the chair from its resting place, took it to Archibald and helped him into it. He was made comfortable and off the pair went, Archibald in his pyjamas and dressing gown and with a plaid shawl about him.

On the Hockley Road, about a mile from the house, the invalid decided that he wanted a cigarette and asked Nurse Mitchell to light it for him, which she did, walking around to the side of the chair to do so. She returned to the rear of the chair and resumed pushing. Hardly had she taken six steps when there was an immense explosion and the chair was a tangled mess of metal. The explosion was so loud that local people thought that it was the start of an unheralded air raid attack, unusual at lunchtime. For Archibald, there was no hope. Nurse Mitchell was flung several feet from the chair and later told police that she heard the sounds of her employer's body parts landing in different areas of the vicinity. Police were to find a left leg fifteen feet up in a tree and its partner forty-eight feet away in a garden. It was a miracle that Nurse Mitchell survived, although she was to walk with a limp for the rest of her life.

Essex Police launched a full enquiry, eventually led by Superintendent George H Totterdell, the head of the CID. It was soon established that the cause of the explosion was a British Number 75 Hawkins grenade, used by British infantry to blow the tracks off of tanks. Unfortunately for Archibald, his son had not only been trained to use the grenade, his barracks at Spilsbury had a store full of them. Doris Brown told police how proud she was of Eric's prowess with things mechanical, saying that he could repair a radio. The police, by now highly suspicious of Eric, carried out tests on similar chairs to see if a pressure plate attached to the base of the chair could be adapted so that it would be activated by the weight of a man, rather than the weight of a tank. They came to the conclusion that it was possible and hauled Eric in for questioning. Eric soon confessed to the murder. According to the *Southend Standard* he said he had decided that the best thing for his father was to 'die mercifully' for making his mother into a

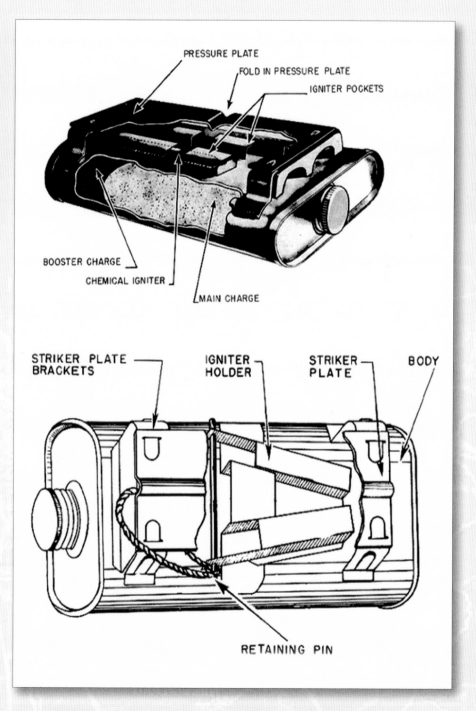

Right: A Hawkins Grenade, used in the Rayleigh Bath Chair Murder, was about 7" x 4" and looked like a large cycle lamp.

drudge. He had therefore stolen the grenade from the store on his base, adjusted the pressure plate and attached it to the bottom of his father's Bath chair. Tony Roles, of the British Ordnance Collectors Network, speculates that Eric Brown made the pressure plate more sensitive, 'probably by partly sawing through the "bridge" on the top with something like a hacksaw.'

Eric was arrested and charged with murder.

On 4 November 1943, at the Essex Assizes at Chelmsford, Eric pleaded not guilty by reason of insanity. One defence doctor stated that he was schizophrenic; in contrast, the prison doctor gave it as his opinion that he was sane. However, this same doctor then pointed out that while awaiting trial, Eric had attempted suicide by trying to cut his own throat. The members of the jury formed their own opinions and found him guilty but insane. He was detained at His Majesty's pleasure, which turned out to be until 1975, when, aged 51 and having spent 32 years in a psychiatric hospital, Eric was released.

The Wigwam Murder

The so-called 'Wigwam Murder' was a celebrated case that caused a sensation at the time. It is well documented by Dr Keith Simpson, the Home Office Pathologist involved in the case, his secretary at the time, Milly Lefebure and Detective Inspector Edward 'Ted' Greeno of Scotland Yard, who led the team of police investigators. The case is mentioned in many of the books written about the era, simply because there were few exotic Red Indians in Britain and fewer wigwams still.

On 7 October 1942, a body was found in the sand dunes on Hankley Common, not far from Godalming in Surrey, by a group of Marines on exercise there. One of them noticed a desiccated hand poking up through the earth. On investigation, part of a leg was also spotted. This was the start of a murder enquiry that involved both the Surrey CID and one of the most famous of the Scotland Yard detectives, Ted Greeno, whose long career was spent covering a myriad of different cases, several mentioned in this book. Greeno was later to say that the Wigwam Murder was 'nearly the perfect crime – a murder not only unsolved, but undiscovered,' (*War on the Underworld*). The *Daily Express* would later call Greeno's work on the case the 'detective achievement of the century.'

Rats had eaten away the thumb and two fingers of the hand and it and the leg were becoming mummified. Death was not recent but not so long ago that disturbed heather, lying upside down in the earth over the grave, had died off. Indeed, it had flowered and was still green, so had not long been disturbed.

The body in the shallow grave was disintegrating and crawling with maggots. Its clothes were female and tatty, a green flowered dress, but not

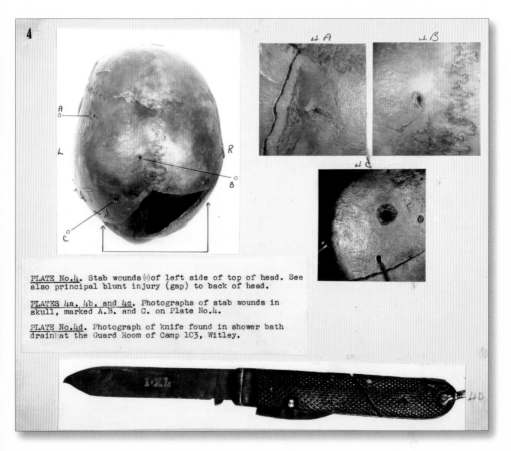

4

PLATE No.4. Stab wounds (•)of left side of top of head. See also principal blunt injury (gap) to back of head.

PLATES 4a, 4b, and 4c. Photographs of stab wounds in skull, marked A.B. and C. on Plate No.4.

PLATE No.4d. Photograph of knife found in shower bath drain at the Guard Room of Camp 103, Witley.

Above: The murder weapon used by August Sangret in 1942, with the distinctive parrot beak end. The wounds inflicted on Joan Pearl Wolfe shattered the victim's skull into thirty-eight pieces. (National Archives, DPP 2/1061 (14))

disarranged. The back of the skull was caved in and the body had been dragged headfirst and put into the grave lying face downwards.

The post mortem at Guy's Hospital proved that the victim had been hit once with a blow so hard that it shattered her skull into thirty-eight pieces. There were also several stab and defensive wounds, all administered during life. The final blow was struck while the victim was lying face down on the ground. Murder had clearly been committed and the weapons were a heavy blunt instrument such as a pole or tree bough and a distinctive implement with a sharp end similar to a parrot beak. The body was that of a nineteen or twenty-year-old girl, with very prominent front teeth and bleached hair. A local police officer, Superintendent Richard Webb, recognised the girl's clothes and the scant description and named her as Joan Pearl Wolfe. She had been in to his office to see him about six weeks before and had said that she was living in an improvised shelter, a wigwam, made of branches and leaves, in the woods. A soldier friend, August Sangret, a Canadian Indian, had built the wigwam for her. Joan had confided to Webb that she was pregnant and he had sent her to hospital. Joan had later discharged herself. Sangret, based at the nearby Witley Camp, had called on Webb too, asking if he knew of Joan's whereabouts. He also said that he wanted to marry her.

The police painstakingly searched for the girl's missing shoes and the murder weapons, her bag having already been located. A knife had been picked up at the same time as the bag but had been thrown away as it was not thought pertinent to the case. A birch wood stake of the exact diameter of the wound in Joan's skull was found. It had hairs attached to it that were later shown to match Joan's and the end was crushed. It was undoubtedly the murder weapon.

Inspector Greeno interviewed Joan's boyfriend, Sangret.

August Sangret was born in Battleford, Saskatchewan on 28 August 1913. He was of mixed parentage, being part French Canadian and part Cree Indian. His early life had been hard and he had missed all of his schooling through illness, with the result that, although he could sign his name, he was otherwise completely illiterate. He had been a farm labourer in Canada in the 1920s, but during the 1930s had convictions for vagrancy and theft, and had served six months in jail for violent assault and a further three months for threatening to shoot a woman. He had a good memory and had learnt some of the traditional crafts of the Cree tribe, including how to make a wigwam shelter as he had done for Joan Wolfe. In June 1940, Sangret had enlisted as a full-time soldier in The Regina Rifle Regiment, from which he was often reported Absent Without Leave. On 13 July 1942, he found himself at Jasper Camp, close to Hankley Common and the town of Godalming, described by Greeno as, "where illiterates from Canada's prairies and backwoods studied three months, and then left."

Right: The panel on the Memorial to the Missing with Sangret's name engraved with other missing Canadian military personnel.

Sangret confirmed that the clothes from the body were Joan's and stated that he had last seen her on 14 September. He did not ask questions about what had happened to Joan but did give Greeno a 17,000-word statement, the longest statement Greeno remembered in a murder hunt, covering fifty-eight pages and taking five days to note down, detailing his dealings with her. During this time, Dr Keith Simpson looked for clues amongst Sangret's belongings to what had happened and who had killed Joan. Although there were suspicious stains on a blanket and on Sangret's battledress trousers, there was no proven link to Joan's murder. Greeno, convinced he had his man, had to let Sangret leave as, although he had guessed that Joan had been found and said that he thought he would get the blame, not one word Sangret had uttered could be used to incriminate him.

It was vital to find the knife with the parrot beak end.

A Canadian soldier, Corporal Crowle, who was picking blackberries on Hankley Common, reported that he had found a black handled knife with a hooked point stuck into a tree near a shack in the woods by the common. He also remembered hearing a man and woman arguing nearby. Greeno later identified the shack as Joan's wigwam. The knife had been taken back to Witley Camp and turned over to the provosts there. In turn, it was passed on to August Sangret. Despite intense searching around the grave site, the knife was not located.

At Witley Camp a month later, the drains had become a problem. When cleared out, the blockage was found to be not just the expected mass of paper and cigarette ends, but also a black handled knife with a hooked blade. Tests later found that the hook exactly fitted wounds in Joan's skull.

Greeno spoke once again to Sangret. Casually dropping the fact that Sangret had said the knife was his to the military police at Witley Camp, Sangret immediately fell into the trap set. Instead of denying all knowledge of the knife, he said that it belonged to Joan, not himself. The pair had used it at the wigwam and he had stuck it into a tree nearby. By hiding it, Sangret was tacitly admitting it had something to do with Joan's death. He was charged with the murder of Joan Pearl Wolfe. "I didn't do it. No, sir. Someone did, but I'll have to take the rap," Greeno reported Sanget as saying at the time.

Seventy-four witnesses were called to the trial. Greeno and his team had interviewed thousands of people to find those witnesses. The case was watertight. Sangret was found guilty at Kingston Assize Court. Before he was hanged at Wandsworth Jail on 29 April 1943, he confessed to killing Joan Pearl Wolfe. When Dr Keith Simpson performed the autopsy, he found the name Pearl tattooed on Sangret's arm.

Sangret's name can be found on the Memorial to the Fallen at Brookwood Cemetery, Surrey (Panel 23, Column 3).

Frustrating

Sometimes, the perpetrator of a crime was not caught, despite the best efforts of some of the finest police and forensic minds of the era. When this happened, it was frustrating for the police and for victims alike.

The Cul-De-Sac Murder

(The author is indebted to former Southampton policeman, Jim Brown, and the Hampshire Police Historical Society for the details of this case and the accompanying photographs.)

Southampton had its share of Victorian working class properties, many of which, if they had survived the slum clearances of the late 1930s, were derelict by the beginning of the 1940s. Exmouth Street was one-such. It was originally a cul-de-sac of twelve terraced houses that were built in the 1830s. A small pedestrian bridge over the railway line linked it to Exmouth Place, where there were twelve similar properties. In 1941, all were dilapidated and haunted only by the area's prostitutes and their clients, undisturbed in the empty buildings and unlit streets. The Bay Tree Inn stood on the corner of the street, at its junction with New Road.

Fourteen-year-old Evelyn Privett, of nearby St Andrews Road, had good reason to ignore the cries coming from Exmouth Street at about 11pm on Monday 12 February. She was out with an American sailor and was desperate for her father not to find out. The pair were walking along the

Above: The site of the Bay Tree Inn, Southampton, today.

upper stretch of New Road and were passing the Bay Tree Inn at its entrance to Exmouth Street when they heard a woman cry out, "Don't kill me, please, please." They continued on their way, ignoring the cry. They then disregarded a scream, which young Evelyn later described, "as if from somebody wanting help." In the darkness they could see nothing. Thinking that perhaps people were, "skylarking," as Evelyn later explained, and not wanting to get involved, the pair hurried on.

A few hundred yards later, the pair met two policemen standing on the corner of New Road, at Six Dials, the meeting point of six nearby roads. They said nothing. Evelyn later explained that she was late home and did not want trouble from her parents. The fact that she was a fourteen-year-old out with an adult American sailor may also have been a factor in the couple's silence. When she later told her mother what she had heard, she was told to be quiet and not to tell anyone, especially her father.

The landlord of the Bay Tree Inn, Peter Reddington, heard a noise outside later that same night as he was going to bed in the upper floor of the premises. He told his wife that he thought there was a fight going on. He heard voices but could not make out what was said. He thought he heard groans, but he took no action. Trouble outside, unfortunately, was, "as usual'.

The following morning, a gruesome discovery was made in the Exmouth Street cul-de-sac.

An ARP driver, Frederick George Edmunds, of Bellemoor Road, was walking towards the Bay Tree Inn, along New Road, at about 8.15am. As he passed the cul-de-sac he noticed what he thought was a mound of rags in the roadway, outside one of the derelict terraced houses, about thirty yards from the junction with New Road.

Peter Cecil Jefferies, aged seventeen, of Bitterne Road, was also walking along New Road on his way to catch a bus to attend Peter Symonds School, Winchester at the same time. He saw Frederick Edmunds walk down Exmouth Street to investigate further. When Edmunds reached the bundle and looked closer he realised that the rags were, in fact, a fake leopard-skin coat that was thrown open, revealing the body of a woman lying on her back with her skirt pushed up high above her waist, exposing her lower body. He sent Peter, who had joined him, to the Civic Centre Police Headquarters, just under a quarter of a mile away, to report the horrific scene.

Detective Inspector (DI) Gordon Baker took charge of the investigation when he arrived at 8.55am. On careful examination of the body, he found bruises on both legs, with a superficial wound on the right knee, where the stocking was torn, and bruise marks around the throat. Her handbag was still slung around her shoulder and had not been touched. It contained just five pence in a purse. It was later found that she had one shilling and nine pence in the pocket of the uniform overall she had been carrying. DI Gordon also noted that an American soldier's olive green forage cap, size seven, was underneath the nape of the victim's neck. The cap was new but had been altered from its original shape. The senior police surgeon, Dr Geoffrey Havers, arrived at the scene at 10am. He considered that she had been dead for less than 24 hours. As it had been raining overnight and the body was lying in a pool of water, a tent was hastily erected over it to protect it.

Professor J.M. Webster, an eminent London pathologist and murder expert, arrived that evening and immediately started work. He carried out a detailed examination of the body with the aid of lighting obtained via a cable run from the nearby Bay Tree Inn. The body was then removed to the public mortuary in Western Esplanade. Here, with Doctor Havers present, Professor Webster conducted a detailed post mortem, lasting two hours. It was completed at midnight. Both doctors agreed that the victim had died from asphyxia, due to manual strangulation, and that she had been sexually assaulted shortly before her death.

In spite of the heavy rain that would have destroyed much of the physical evidence, it was decided to employ bloodhounds in an attempt to trace the owner of the cap found under the body. Newspapers, which had reported the murder, now picked up on this more traditional method of chasing down a fugitive, with reports from as far away as Nottingham mentioning the fact that blood hounds were on the scent (*Nottingham Evening Post*, Monday 19 February 1945). Nina Elms, a friend of one of the investigating police officers, was taken to the scene with her two bloodhounds, Minstral and Magda, who were given the cap. They then toured the area. They also visited several of the American military establishments in the town. The authorities fully co-operated and specially ordered parades were held, supervised by military police. It was hoped that the bloodhounds may have been able to recognise any individual to connect him with the cap and to see if any soldier had fresh scratch marks, but this proved to be unsuccessful.

> **In spite of the heavy rain that would have destroyed much of the physical evidence, it was decided to employ bloodhounds in an attempt to trace the owner of the cap found under the body.**

Clearly, DI Gordon Baker had come to the conclusion that the person responsible was an American G.I. who had left his cap behind in the confusion of his attack and escape. Subsequent enquiries showed that the cap may have been the victim's, although this was never fully established.

The American forces took the possibility of one of their number being involved in the crime seriously and, after representations by the Chief Constable Fred Tarry, were involved in the investigation from the outset. Six

U.S. officers assisted DI Baker and his investigating team of seven detectives. A uniformed American military policeman thus assisted a uniformed police constable in remaining at the scene to protect it until such time as the initial enquiries were completed.

The victim was identified as 55-year-old Mary Helen Hoyles, known as Helen, employed for the previous nine months to make sandwiches at the American Red Cross Club in the High Street. She had left the club at 10.40pm on the night of the murder and, as usual, walked along Above Bar and turned down New Road.

The American Red Cross Club provided transport for staff finishing late at night, but Miss Hoyles never used this facility because she lived nearby. The 1935 to 1941 Southampton Street Directories record Miss Helen Hoyles, shopkeeper, as living at 28 New Road, just a few yards from the Bay Tree Inn at number 10. However, the block of houses that included number 28 in New Road, were destroyed in the blitz on the night of 23 November 1940. Miss Hoyles had therefore rented two rooms at 40 New Road from Miss Irene Adams. She would normally walk past the entrance of Exmouth Street en route to her home from work at the American Red Cross.

Miss Hoyles was a single woman, the daughter of James Hoyles, a general labourer from Devon. She was said to be an enigmatic woman who, although she had lived in Southampton for many years, had almost no friends and few knew her well. Those who did said she was a quiet unassuming woman who 'kept herself to herself', and 'a pleasant little woman and a good worker'.

However, at the inquest on 17 August, when enquiries had been virtually completed, witnesses came forward to talk of Miss Hoyles' association with American servicemen. This gave a different impression of the victim. John Watts, of Wilton Street, worked on the same shift as Miss Hoyles when he was a kitchen hand in the American Red Cross Club. He had seen her in South Front (in the near vicinity of Exmouth Street) at 10.30pm on 1 February when an American soldier was holding her arm. The soldier was white with fair hair.

Police Sergeant Charlie Rhodes spoke of an incident involving Miss Hoyles that he witnessed on a night at the end of the week ending 2 February. Whilst on duty, he heard laughing and giggling coming from the blitzed ruins of Holy Trinity Church. He entered the ruined building by a side door, shone his torch and found Miss Hoyles "in a compromising position". Miss Hoyles gave her details, when requested, and the soldier voluntarily produced his identity card. His name was "Polish sounding" and began with the letters "Mach". Miss Hoyles was distressed and produced some coins from her handbag and tried to give them to the sergeant, saying "Take this, take this." She was told that persons offering bribes were liable to be arrested and she was allowed to go on her way with the soldier.

One witness, Woodrow Gunnells, a private in the U.S. Army, made a significant statement. He was in Above Bar at about 10.45pm on the night of the murder when he saw Miss Hoyles, whom he identified from a subsequent photograph. She was walking on the pavement on the east side of the road, between Hanover Buildings and Pound Tree Road. A white American soldier, a private who was wearing a light field jacket and overseas cap, accompanied her. He was about twenty-four or twenty-five years of age, about 5' 8" tall with light hair. He at first appeared drunk, as he staggered as the witness passed them, but Private Gunnells said he would not be able to identify him if he saw him again. It was this statement, coupled with the finding of the forage cap, which concentrated police enquiries on attempting to trace this individual, who became a prime suspect.

The police also widely circulated Miss Hoyle's description in an effort to trace witnesses who may have seen her, accompanied by a man. It was given as 5' 4", medium build, medium brown hair and hatless. She was wearing a fake leopard skin coat with a small American Red Cross badge pinned to the lapel, a greenish coloured scarf, dark blue woollen frock, stockings, low heeled shoes with green uppers and yellow piping. She was carrying a small brown leather shopping bag with drawstrings and an overall of blue-grey material with the American Red Cross insignia on the left sleeve. On the seventh day of the investigation the police issued a description of the white

American soldier who had been seen in her company at 10.45pm the night she left work. He fitted the description of an American soldier seen with her on 1 February in the Robert Burns public house in South Front and who had been said to have "staring eyes". This last was reported widely in the newspapers at the time.

Because of the American military connection, and representations by the Chief Constable, Fred Tarry, the American forces assisted in making large scale enquiries, not only at military units in this country but those abroad. The *Gloucester Echo* (22 February 1945) reported that efforts were being made to trace a soldier, believed to be a sergeant, who had 'blue penetrating eyes'.

Above: The Cul-de-sac Murder, Chief Constable Fred Tarry.

At this period there were many movements of military personnel through the town, returning from active service and then departing for home or other units. The war in Europe was almost over and VE Day

(Victory in Europe Day) was only three months away, on 8 May 1945. The logistical problems of ascertaining the movements of an individual were therefore enormous.

The subsequent inquest jury on Wednesday 15 August predictably returned a verdict of "Murder by some person or persons unknown" and although police enquiries continued for some time, the case remained unsolved. The *Gloucester Citizen* states that over forty police forces were involved in the hunt for Miss Hoyles' murderer (16 August 1945). In 1947, DI Gordon Baker and Chief Superintendent Harry Kemble visited Germany to interview an American soldier who was in prison in Mannheim. He had been in Southampton at the material time and was now serving a 10-year sentence for manslaughter. He had been originally charged with murder after strangling a German woman, but he could not be connected and the matter remained unresolved.

However, later that year, following a reappraisal of the evidence, it was realised that Miss Hoyle was not wearing a hat when her body was found. This, in an age when a lady was not dressed if she was not wearing a hat when out in public, was unusual. It was then belatedly realised that she owned a similar garrison cap to the one she was found with, that she sometimes wore for fun. Therefore, the discarded cap found at the scene could possibly have been hers. DNA testing, which would have settled the matter once and for all, was still a long way off. With this realisation, a different suspect then came to light.

It was believed that the killer, in what had become known as the "Cul-de-Sac Murder", was, in fact, a British merchant seaman who lived in the nearby Seaman's Hostel in Oxford Street. On the night of the murder he had not slept in his bed. He had figured in earlier enquiries but been dropped when it was thought that the murderer was an American serviceman. By the time the link was established it was too late. He had died in a drowning accident at sea. His body was later found floating in the Channel.

Percy Chislett – Shot in an Alley

(The author is indebted to former Southampton policeman, Jim Brown, and the Hampshire Police Historical Society for the details of this case and the accompanying photographs.)

Military rules, regulations and laws sometimes got in the way of bringing justice, despite the willingness of authorities to co-operate. Such was the case of an unfortunate naval rating, at the very end of the war.

What should have been a time for jubilation, the end of hostilities after six long years of war, were marred in Southampton by the murder of a sailor, Percy Chislett, who was shot dead on Thursday 30 August, 1945.

St George's Street, in central Southampton, was a short cul-de-sac leading from Houndwell, adjacent to Hoglands Park, with a small pedestrian alley at the end leading to the bustling shopping area of East Street. Much of the property in the area, including what had been a huge Edwin Jones department store, had been razed to the ground in the blitz.

At 11pm on Thursday 30 August 1945, neighbours heard what sounded like a gunshot. The blood-soaked body of a sailor was then found, lying on the ground at the junction of St George's Street and the alley.

The senior police surgeon, Dr G.G. Havers, attended the scene, together with Detective Inspector Gordon Baker, who led the police enquiries. Dr Havers confirmed that the deceased had been shot from the front, in the chest, with the bullet leaving from under his left shoulder. There was no sign of the pistol used in the shooting, although a bullet and spent cartridge case were found at the scene.

From door to door enquiries it was revealed that just prior to the shooting voices of a woman and two men were heard laughing and talking, and immediately after the noise of the shot a man said, "Come on, get up." Shortly afterwards, the sound of heavy footsteps were heard running down the alley towards East Street.

The sailor was twenty-nine-year-old Percy Chislett, a married British naval rating from Heart's Delight, Trinity Bay, Newfoundland, who was serving on a Royal Navy tug in Southampton Water. He had been based in the town for the previous ten days. Police were able to piece together Chislett's last movements up to a point. He had left his ship at 8pm that evening, in the company of another naval rating. He had been with two recently met friends in a local public house in the Bevois Valley area of the town, but had left at 10.30pm intending to rejoin his ship. He was last seen in the Six Dials area, the meeting point of several major arteries through Southampton. This was a short distance from St George's Street, which was not the direct route back to his ship. Extensive enquiries were made but they led nowhere and the case was considered to be unsolved. Despite appeals in the local press, none of the witnesses came forward and DI Baker believed that a love rival had shot the unfortunate sailor. Local newspapers, following the story, report that, despite questioning more than 150 people, the police could not find the culprit and an inquest jury returned an open verdict. (*Dundee Courier*, 8 January 1946).

The local *Southern Evening Echo* published a story more than two years later concerning another unsolved murder in 1945, that of Helen Hoyles. As a direct result of this coverage, PC 'Wally' Tate overheard a conversation about the Chislett murder in a public house. This was sufficiently important to be reported to Detective Inspector Hugh O'Conner, who was able to obtain new evidence from previously uncooperative witnesses. This clearly established that an American serviceman was responsible for Chislett's murder. Under the American Armed Forces Act if this person was still serving he could have appeared before a United States court martial and been punished for the murder on British soil. However, he was now a civilian resident in the United States of America as he had been discharged after the war. After intensive discussion, the legal authorities eventually ruled that he could not be extradited to the United Kingdom to stand trial and as a civilian he was not eligible for a court martial. In December 1947, the Home Office directed that the Chislett murder be treated as 'closed'. Frustratingly, the murderer got away with his crime.

Above: Percy Chislett was buried in Hollybrook Cemetery on 5 September 1945, with a War Graves Commission headstone in plot M12/032 It states, P. Chislett of Newfoundland, Seaman LT/JX 315669, Royal Naval Patrol Service, 30th August 1945 aged 29.

Crimes committed by service personnel during the Second World War were as varied as by their civilian counterparts. They are more shocking as those in uniform are put into a position of trust, whether that trust is wanted or warranted, or not. The general public looks to its military personnel for protection in time of need and a breach of this trust stands out as a betrayal that is hard to forgive, no matter what the cause.

PREVENT ROAD ACCIDENTS!

cross with the lights especially during the

BLACKOUT

but look out for turning traffic

Above: The blackout was vital to shield Britain from her overhead enemies but it was a six-year opportunity for those with criminal intent. While the authorities were busy prosecuting the public for blackout infringements, the unscrupulous took full advantage.

Epilogue

In late 2015 and early 2016, the Museum of London staged an exhibition of items from the Metropolitan Police's Crime Museum, the so-called 'Black Museum,' which is not open to the general public. The museum houses a collection of items related to cases investigated by the Metropolitan Police since its inception in 1829. The exhibition attracted thousands of people interested in hearing about the work of the Met.

Amongst its exhibits were the death masks from offenders hanged outside Newgate Prison, including 'the Edgeware Road Murderer' James Greenacre, who was hanged on 2 May 1837 for murdering his fiancée, Hannah Brown, and Franz Muller, who committed the railway's first recorded murder, that of Thomas Briggs, and who was hanged on 14 November 1864. The masks show ordinary men, serene in death, none of them giving any clue to their notoriety or crime.

Also amongst the exhibits were the ropes used to execute a number of murderers. The row of nooses was a sobering sight. They were each labelled with the name and crime of the person whose life they had ended. Amongst these was Amelia Dyer, the fifty-seven-year-old 'baby farmer,' who looked after unwanted babies for payment. She was hanged in 1896 for the murder of a two-month old girl, Doris Marmon. Six more tiny bodies were recovered from the Thames at the same time as that of little Doris. Once again, the ropes looked ordinary, the knotted loops being the only clue to the use they had been put to.

Amongst the later exhibits were some of the items recovered in the Blackout Ripper Murders by Gordon Cummins. These were Greeno's jigsaw puzzle pieces. They included table knives, a razorblade and a can opener, all very mundane objects. It is a shock to think that the blunt-looking, rounded-end blades on the bone handled dinner knives were used, along with the razor blade and the wickedly pointed can opener, by the RAF flyer with the refined voice to mutilate his victims.

The ordinary comes into play throughout this book. In wartime, even a kitchen sink has a value to someone who has lost theirs. Ordinary people were placed into extraordinary times and expected to step up, carry on and not make a fuss. For the majority, this was precisely what they did. However, the mad, the bad and the weak took the opportunities circumstances presented and, soon, the ordinary became the notorious, the whispered of or the shamed.

Crime is always intriguing and none more so than that perpetrated during this most pressing of times, the Second World War.

Bibliography

Books

Allen, RE., *The Concise Oxford Dictionary, Eight Edition* (Clarendon Press, Oxford, 1991)

Bechhofer Roberts, CE., (*The Trial of Jones and Hulten*, Jarrolds Publishers (London) Limited, London, 1945)

Calder. A., *The People's War,* (The Literary Guild, 1969)

Croall. J., *Don't You Know There's A War On?* (The History Press, Stroud, 1989)

Dunboyne. Lord, Ed., *The Trial of John George Haigh (The Acid Bath Murderer)* (William Hodge and Company, Limited, London, Edinburgh, Glasgow, 1953)

Fabian, R., *Fabian of the Yard* (The Naldrett Press Ltd., Kingswood, 1950)

Fowler, HW and Fowler, FG, *the Concise Oxford Dictionary of Current English* (Clarendon Press, Oxford, 1991)

Fraser, F., and Morton, J., *Mad Frank and Friends* (Little, Brown and Company, London, 1998)

Fraser, F., and Morton, J., *Mad Frank's Diary, A Chronicle of the Life of Britain's Most Notorious Villain* (Virgin Publishing Ltd., London, 2000)

Gardiner, J., *Wartime Britain 1939 – 1945* (Headline Book Publishing, London, 2004)

Glass, C., *Deserter, The Last Untold Story of the Second World War* (Harper Press, London, 2013)

Goodall, F., *Voices from the Home Front* (David & Charles, Newton Abbott, 2004)

Greeno. E., *War on the Underworld* (John Long, London, 1960)

Hodge, S., *The Home Front in World War Two, Keep Calm and Carry On* (Pen & Sword Books Ltd., Barnsley, 2012)

Ingleton, R., *The Gentlemen at War, Policing Britain 1939-45* (Cranborne Publications, Maidstone, 1994)

Kennedy. L., *10 Rillington Place* (Victor Gollancz Ltd, London, 1961)

Kirby, Dick., *The Guv'nors* (Wharncliffe True Crime, Barnsley, 2010)

Leete., J., *The New Forest at War* (Sabrestorm Publishing, Sevenoaks, 2014)

Lefebure. M., *Murder on the Home Front* (Heinemann Books, 1954, ISIS Publishing Ltd., Oxford, 2014 edition)

Legg. P., *Folklore of Hampshire* (The History Press, 2010)

Legg. P. & Marsh. J., A 1950s *Southampton Childhood* (The History Press, 2013)

Leslie, D., *Banged Up* (Black & White Publishing, Edinburgh, 2014

Lewis, P., *A People's War* (Methuen, London, 1986)

Longmate, N., (Ed.) *The Home Front An Anthology 1938-1945* (Chatto & Windus Ltd., London, 1981)

Marston. E., *John Christie*, (The National Archives, Kew, 2007)

Minns, R., *Bombers & Mash* (Virago, London, 1980, 2012 edition)

Moorhouse, R., *Berlin at War, Life and Death in Hitler's Capital 1939-45* (The Bodley Head, London, 2010)

Mortimer, G., *The Longest Night 10-11May 1941, Voices from the London Blitz* (Orion Books Ltd., London, 2005)

Nicholson, V., *Millions Like Us Women's Lives in War and Peace 1939-1945* (Viking, London, 2011)

Nixon, B., *Raiders Overhead* (Scolar Press, London, 1980)

Orwell, G., *Shooting an Elephant* (Secker and Warburg, London, 1950)

Read, S., *The Blackout Murders* (JR Books, London, 2006)

Read, S., *Dark City, Crime in Wartime London* (Ian Allan Publishing, Hersham, 2010)

Simpson CBE, K., *Forty Years of Murder An Autobiography* (George G Harrap & Co. Ltd., London, 1978)

Thomas, D., *An Underground at War* (John Murray (Publishers), London, 2003

Trow, M.J., *War Crimes Underworld Britain in the Second World War* (Pen & Sword Military, Barnsley, 2008)

Websites

23rd Sussex Home Guard: *www.sussexhomeguard.co.uk*

BBC: *www.bbc.co.uk/news/magazine-20160819*

news.*bbc.co.uk/onthisday/hi/dates/stories/june/25/newsid_3721000/3721267.s tm*

Black Kalendar: *www.blackkalendar.nl/*

Blitz Walkers: *blitzwalkers.blogspot.co.uk*

British Newspaper Archive: *www.britishnewspaperarchive.co.uk/*

British Ordnance Collectors Network: *www.bocn.co.uk*

Café de Paris: *www.cafedeparis.com*

Capital Punishment UK: *www.capitalpunishmentuk.org/sheptonm.html*

Dreadnought Project: *www.dreadnoughtproject.org/tfs/index.php/Ralph_Douglas_Binney#cite_n ote-3*

Heretical: *www.heretical.com/british/joyce*

History Stack Exchange: *history.stackexchange.com/questions/15237/rape-perpetrated-by-american-soldiers-during-wwii*

The Ivor Novello Appreciation Society: *www.ivornovello.com*

KZWP: *www.kzwp.com/lyons/*

London Remembers: *www.londonremembers.com*

Measuring Worth: *www.measuringworth.com*

Murderpedia: *murderpedia.org*

Murder UK: *www.murderuk.com*

National Crime Syndicate: *www.nationalcrimesyndicate.com*

New Forest Life: *www.newforest-life.com/WW2-Breamore-Patton.html*

Primary Homework Help: *www.primaryhomeworkhelp.co.uk*

Prison History:
   www.prisonhistory.co.uk/shepton_mallet_prison_360_years_.htm

Safran-Arts: *www.safran-arts.com/*

Spartacus: *spartacus-educational.com*

Telegraph: *www.telegraph.co.uk/news/obituaries/10001457/Molly-Lefebure.html*

The Week: *www.theweek.co.uk/politics/3149/nation-looters-it-even-happened-blitz#ixzz3RdADHEHR*

Victoria and Albert Museum: *www.vam.ac.uk*

Wikipedia: *en.wikipedia.org*

Zionism Isreal: *www.zionism-israel.com*

Acknowledgements

There are always a great number of people to thank when producing a book of this nature. I hope I haven't forgotten anyone! If I have, please accept my sincere thanks. I could not have written this book without you.

Special thanks to:

Ian Bayley, Sabrestorm Publishing, my commissioning editor.
    Ian, thank you for your patience and understanding.

Mick Barry and the Essex Police Museum.

Neil Bright and Steve Hunnisett – Blitzwalkers.

Jim Brown, former Southampton City Police Officer, and author.
    Thank you for sharing.

Caroline Brodrick, for sharing her family's memories of Ralph
    Binney, CBE.

Peter Clarke, for allowing me to photograph his British Free Corps
    jacket.

James Cross, West Midlands Police Museum.

Christine Donovan, for her support when it was needed.

Alison Fletcher, Office Manager, Senior Command Suite, South
    Yorkshire Police.

Hampshire Constabulary Historical Society.

John Leete, for staunch support and advice at the beginning.

Purple Joe Legg, for pointing me in the right direction and for talking
    to the right people.

James Marsh, for allowing me to use his wartime memories.

Erica and Roy Montgomery, for their help with illustrations.

Michael O'Bryne, Chief Constable of Bedfordshire Police (retired),
    for his advice and guidance and for not turning me down when
    I asked if he would write the Foreword.

Tony Roles, British Ordnance Collectors Network, for his expert help
    and advice.

Craig Timmins, www.nationalcrimesyndicate.com

Richard Hunt and the 23rd Sussex Home Guard.

Wouter Brasse and Ruth Isseroff, zionism-israel.com

The manager and staff at the Café de Paris, London.

The fantastically helpful staff at The National Archives.

The curator and staff at Brooklands Museum, Weybridge.

The staff at the Aldershot Military Museum.

The staff at the *Aldershot News*.

The wonderful librarians at The British Library and the following local libraries: Aldershot, Farnborough, Southampton Central, Woolston, Waterlooville.

The Writing Buddies, for their support and suggestions – thanks, everyone!

And last, but certainly not least, my husband Joe, who patiently waits for me in the present, while I am busy delving into the past.

Above: Make Do and Mend became a way of life for millions during the war. However, there were times when this just would not do. Precious clothing coupons were spent on ready-made clothing, cut to the official utility patterns to conserve cloth, or were used to buy material for the dressmaker. Of course, both the coupons and the cloth became targets for theft and black market exploitation.

Picture Credits

1940s Society at www.1940.co.uk: Inside cover rear flap, front cover, pages 1, 3, 6, 8, 11, 16, 17, 19, 20, bottom 21, 26, 30, 32, 35, 40, 43, 50, 59, 62, 102, 107, 108, 113, 115, 150 and 156

Alamy: Pages 4, 77, 81, 84 and 92

Aldershot Advertiser: Page 53

Aldershot News: Page 127

Brooklands Museum: Top page 21

Ian Bayley: 67 and 107

Caroline Brodrick: Page 66

Jim Brown: Pages 100, 142 and 149

Peter Clarke: Page 118

Sheila Hayward: Pages 33 and 37

Legg collection: inside cover rear flap, bottom page 15, 97, 121, 129, 130 and 140

James Marsh: Page 34

Roy Montgomery: Page 104

National Archives: Pages 23, 57, 95 and 139,

Navy Department of Ordnance, Washington DC: Page 137

Southampton Police Collection at Southampton Archives, courtesy of Jim Brown: Main page 98, 99 and 146

South Yorkshire Police: Page 70

Craig Timmins at www.nationalcrimesyndicate.com: Page 45

Wikimedia Commons: Page 121

Whilst every effort has been made to trace copyright holders, the sources of some pictures are obscure. The author will gladly make good in future editions any mistakes or omissions brought to her attention.

Index

A

Acid Bath Murderer: 76 - 82
Air Raid: 9, 14, 17, 18, 20, 21, 22, 27,
    41, 51, 52, 53, 59, 71, 94, 104, 115,
    136
Air Raid Siren: 9, 18, 53
Air Raid Precautions (ARP)
    Warden: 52
Air Ministry: 51, 112, 114, 116
Aldershot: 126, 127, 128, 129, 130,
    131
Amery, John: 118, 120
Army: 8, 24, 42, 45, 60, 72, 73, 74,
    83, 105, 115, 120, 126, 127, 131,
    132, 133, 134
Auxiliary Fire Service: 28

B

Bath Chair Murder: 135, 137
Berkeley, Ballard: 25
Bevin Boys: 36, 37
Bevin, Earnest: 36
Binney Award: 69, 70
Binney, Capt Ralph Douglas: 66, 67,
    68, 69, 70, 71, 154
Blackout: 8, 10, 20, 23, 27, 37, 51,
    52, 53, 54, 60, 61, 64, 94
Blackout Ripper: 55, 57, 58, 150
Black Museum: 150
Blitz: 13, 17, 18, 22, 24, 25, 26, 41,
    85, 103, 145, 148
Board of Trade: 39, 41, 42, 47, 48
Borstal: 10, 108, 110, 111
Breamore House: 126
Brodrick, Caroline: 66, 69, 70,
    154
Brown, Jim 97, 142, 147, 154
Burglary: 104
Butcher Gangs: 41

C

Cafe de Paris: 22, 23, 24, 25, 154
Canadian Riots: 126
Careless Talk: 108
Christie, John Reginald Halliday:
    82 - 93
Cleft Chin Murder: 132
Clothing Coupons: 37, 104, 106
Cherrill, Frederick: 55, 56
Chichester: 39, 108
Churchill, Winston: 28
Conscription: 123, 135
Coventry13-15
Cummins, Gordon: 55, 57, 60, 150

D

D-Day: 13, 128
Defence Regulations:14, 108
Dead End Kids: 114
Deserters: 8, 42, 44, 45
Diamonds: 47, 48
Dig for Victory: 34
Dobkin, Harry: 93-97
Dover: 18
Duncan, Helen: 120-121

E

Espionage: 116
Evans, Timothy John 86-90, 93

F

Folkstone: 60
Fraud: 5, 57, 80, 91, 103 - 105, 112,
    121
Fraser, Frank: 40, 109

G

Genovese, Vito: 45
Glass, Charles: 44, 114, 131

Goodall, Felicity: 26, 37, 53, 104, 115, 126
Great Western Railway: 42
Greeno, Edward (Ted): 46, 56 - 58, 60, 65, 71, 72, 138, 140, 141, 150

H
Haigh, John George: 76-82
Hamilton, Evelyn: 56, 59, 60
Hedley, Bobby: 40
Hedley, Ronald: 68, 71
Heyward, Mary: 58, 60
Higgins, Robert: 75, 76
Hitler: 7, 9, 76, 85, 118, 120, 131
Home Guard: 21, 22, 25, 41
Hoisters: 109
Home front: 9, 10, 13, 14, 21, 26, 29, 31, 37, 52, 53, 61, 63, 80, 104
Hooch: 102, 116
Hull: 13, 49, 105
Hulten, Karl Gustav: 132-135

I
Ingleton, Roy: 14, 27, 28, 39, 42, 109

J
Jewish Haganah: 114
Jones, Elizabeth Maud: 132-135
Johnson, Ken 'Snake Hips': 24, 24
Jouannet, Doris: 58, 59
Joyce, William: 119, 120

K
Kendall, Alan: 25
Kennedy, Ludovic: 83, 85, 87, 90

L
London: 9, 11, 13, 16, 18, 20 - 22, 24 - 26, 37, 40 - 42, 46, 52, 54 - 56, 61, 65, 67 - 69, 75, 81, 83, 85,86, 88, 93,105, 109, 112, 116, 119, 125,

133, 135,144,
Longmate, Norman: 14
Looter: 10, 14, 16, 17, 18, 21, 25-29
Lord Haw-Haw: 119-120
Leckey, Dennis: 61
Leeds: 17, 28, 114, 116
Lefebure, Molly: 63, 94, 138
Lewis, Peter: 17, 18
London Underground: 11, 41, 83
Luftwaffe: 13
Lyons Corner House: 56, 74, 75, 90, 133

M
MacDougall, Philip: 39
Make Do and Mend: 9, 37, 106
Marsh, James: 38, 43, 154
Marston, Edward: 86, 87, 89, 90, 92
Mass Observation: 28
Messina Brothers: 54
Ministry of Food: 38, 39, 48
Ministry of Fuel and Power: 37
Ministry of Labour: 105
Ministry of Supply: 112-114
Ministry of Transport: 41
Minns, Raynes: 18, 42, 43
Morrison, Herbert: 28, 116
Mortimer, Gavin: 18, 25, 27, 41
Mosley, Oswald: 119
Murder: 5, 7, 10, 17, 39, 45, 52 - 65, 67, 68, 71-74, 76-82, 85 87, 89-95, 97, 99, 101, 123- 125, 131-142, 145-150
Murder Squad: 56
Museum of London: 150

N
NAAFI: 39
National Assistance Office: 104
New Forest, The: 126
Nixon, Barbara: 9, 18, 26, 27

Novello, Ivor: 109

O

O'Bryne, Michael: 5, 8, 150
Oatley, Evelyn: 56, 60
Obscene Photographs: 106, 107
O'Dwyer, Phyllis: 58
Old Bailey: 28, 60, 61, 65, 72, 74, 76, 89, 93, 97, 107, 117, 118, 120, 133
Orwell, George: 131

P

Patton, General: 45, 126
Petrol Coupons: 41, 42, 111, 112
Pierrepoint, Albert: 118, 124
Pierrepoint, Tom: 124
Portsmouth: 27, 97, 120, 121
Poulsen, Martinus: 23, 25
Price, Marjorie: 24
Prostitution: 8, 53, 54, 56, 91

R

Racketeering: 8, 48
RAF: 55. 58, 60, 115, 116
Ration Books: 32, 38, 39, 44, 45
Rationing: 8, 10, 22, 29, 31, 33, 36, 49, 112
Read, Simon: 10, 18, 26, 52, 55
Rillington Place: 83, 85, 86, 88, 89, 91, 93
Robbery: 8, 49, 65, 67
Rowan and Maine: 7
Royal Navy: 66, 101, 113, 148

S

Sabini Brothers: 46
Sabrestorm Publishing: 4, 9, 154, 155
Sangret, August: 139-141
Scotland Yard: 7, 46, 55, 56, 74, 107, 138

Shepton Mallet: 122, 124, 125
Simpson, (Cedric) Keith: 60, 61, 82, 94, 138, 141
Slater, Stefan: 54
Soho: 54
Southampton: 13, 43, 97, 98, 99, 101, 106, 142, 145, 147, 148
Spilsbury, Bernard: 56, 57, 58
Spiv: 41, 42, 43
Storer, Edgar: 14
Supermarine: 13

T

The Forty Thieves: 109
Theft: 8, 22, 39, 40, 41, 42, 45, 46, 49, 103, 105, 112, 113, 114, 115, 140
Thomas, Donald: 17, 54, 115
Tratsart, Jack: 75,76
Traylor, Caroline Ellen: 60
Treachery: 103, 117

U

Utility Clothing: 106

V

Vosper Thornycroft: 13

W

Webb, Duncan: 55
Walsall: 14, 42
War Damage Bill: 105
War Damage Commission: 104, 106
Wigwam Murder: 138
Witchcraft: 121
Woolston: 13, 154

Z

Zionists: 114